A Cultural Approach to Populism

This book is a critical introduction of theorisations and research on contemporary political populism emphasising the cultural perspective. It introduces the basic theories and analyses the cultural construction of populism regarding radical democratic theory and empirical studies.

Applying Ernesto Laclau's and Chantal Mouffe's theories, the author builds a bridge between radical democratic and ideational approaches on populism with examples and studies that emphasise European radical right populism, alongside the United States, Latin American and Asian cases. Special attention is paid to relationships between populism and democracy and between populism and media. The contemporary appeal of populism is linked to current developments in welfare states and in global economic and cultural trends. The future of populism is discussed in regard to COVID-19 pandemic and Donald Trump's fall in the US presidential elections in 2020 that together with abovementioned global megatrends and with the development of media and communication environment set conditions for the 2020s populism.

Scholars and students of political science, media and communication studies, cultural studies and social sciences will find this a unique and novel approach.

Juha Herkman is Professor of Media and Communication Studies at the University of Helsinki.

"Herkman has written a comprehensive analysis of populism that interrogates its cultural aspects in order to produce a novel explanation of its appeal. His argument is theory-based and draws examples from various countries. The book brings into dialogue various analytical and conceptual streams from political science, sociology and communication studies. This is an important contribution to a burgeoning literature on the subject".

Silvio R. Waisbord, *Director and Professor, School of Media and Public Affairs, The George Washington University, USA*

"The spectre of authoritarian populism is haunting the halls of democracy posing urgent challenges to our understanding of contemporary politics. Drawing on a wide range of sources Herkman offers a comprehensive guide to contending approaches combining research on the organisation of populist parties and movements with cultural analysis of the emotionally resonant symbols and narratives employed to construct populist identities. Accessible, and provocative. This a book to enjoy and argue with".

Graham Murdock, *Emeritus Professor of Culture and Economy, Loughborough University, UK*

A Cultural Approach to Populism

Juha Herkman

Routledge
Taylor & Francis Group
LONDON AND NEW YORK

First published 2022
by Routledge
2 Park Square, Milton Park, Abingdon, Oxon OX14 4RN

and by Routledge
605 Third Avenue, New York, NY 10158

Routledge is an imprint of the Taylor & Francis Group, an informa business

British Library Cataloguing-in-Publication Data
A catalogue record for this book is available from the British Library

Library of Congress Cataloging-in-Publication Data
A catalog record has been requested for this book

ISBN: 978-1-032-21252-4 (hbk)
ISBN: 978-1-032-21255-5 (pbk)
ISBN: 978-1-003-26753-9 (ebk)

DOI: 10.4324/9781003267539

Typeset in Times New Roman
by KnowledgeWorks Global Ltd.

Contents

Figures and tables

Figures

Tables

Acknowledgements

My interest in populism was sparked roughly a decade ago when I wrote a Finnish academic textbook on the relationship between politics and the media. In the book, I studied the relationship between entertainment media and politics in particular, and populism was found to be a presence in both the research literature and in my case studies. Thereafter, I decided to study populism in depth and received funding from the Academy of Finland to do so in two projects: Representations of the Nordic populism (2013–2018) and Mainstreaming populism in the 21st century (2017–2021). I am very grateful to the Academy of Finland for funding my populism research and to all my colleagues in those projects that have helped me to figure out the mystery of populism during the last 10 years.

This book is a modified translation of my most recent Finnish academic textbook about populism. The translation of the Finnish book was started in 2019 by Paul Hayes with the first two chapters, but unfortunately, he could not continue the project further. I was very busy with other projects and almost forgot the translation. However, in late 2020, I found time and started to translate the rest of the book myself. I also found that I had to update the manuscript because of the COVID-19 pandemic and Donald Trump's fall in the US presidential election in 2020. The raw translation was completed in the beginning of 2021, after which I asked Mark Shackleton to proofread the manuscript. Finally, with Mark's careful help, I could finish the task in February 2021. I am extremely grateful to Paul and Mark for their expertise in English and their dedication to my translation project. I want to also thank Routledge for taking my manuscript into their programme and the four anonymous referees whose comments helped me to develop the manuscript further.

When I started my research on the topic, populism was being studied, but it was not a subject on everyone's lips. Populism has now become a very popular research subject because of Brexit and Donald Trump, which strongly directed minds of Anglo-American researchers to the subject. During the translation of this book, political populism and research do not appear to show signs of abating. Hopefully, my textbook will contribute to understanding the current chameleon-like and nebulous nature of populism.

Helsinki, 15 October 2021
Juha Herkman

Introduction

By the end of 2016, populism had re-entered the world's lexicon as a buzzword and was being repeated at all levels of society. The concept first gained in currency in June of that year when the United Kingdom and Northern Ireland held an advisory referendum and surprisingly voted to "Brexit" – leave the European Union (EU). A significant factor in the result of the referendum was the campaign led by the United Kingdom Independence Party (UKIP) and its anti-EU machinations and nationalist campaign, which has largely been termed populist. Of course, Britain had ground favourable to leaving the EU as Euroscepticism had long been strong in the country, nor did Britain join the eurozone or participate at the heart of the European Union to the same extent as France and Germany (e.g. Leconte 2010, 99). Most of all though, the UKIP leader Nigel Farage became the scourge of the EU, giving criticism of it a public face via colourful political performances of some notoriety.

The election of Donald Trump as President of the United States at the end of 2016 generated even more surprise. The mere rise of Trump as a Republican candidate for president provoked great astonishment and few believed the business billionaire's methods would lead him to most powerful office in the "free world". However, Trump's populist campaign appealed to voters in those blue-collar states where his rival Hillary Clinton should have been strong. Trump promised to "make America great again" by emphasising national industry and business, increasing both border and immigration control, invoking national security and reducing state spending on social security. Trump represented a complete opposite to two-time President Barack Obama, who had promoted equality and multiculturalism as well as environmental programmes. Trump appealed to those disappointed by the Obama administration and succeeded in portraying Clinton as

DOI: 10.4324/9781003267539-1

a representative of a corrupt elite, generating media publicity with his populist messages on Twitter.

Brexit and Trump became global media phenomena, sparking an unprecedented debate on populism. However, populism had been debated in Europe throughout the 21st century. In many western European countries, radical right-wing political parties had been successful in recent elections. They were loudly opposed to immigration and Islamic culture entering Europe's national cultures. Perhaps surprisingly, such parties found footholds, especially in liberal democracies like the Netherlands, Belgium, Austria, Switzerland and the Nordic countries, where issues have traditionally been decided by a broad consensus and where equality, minority rights and the idea of a welfare state have arguably been taken furthest in the world. Pim Fortuyn, who was assassinated in the Netherlands in 2002, formed his own anti-Islamic party – Pim Fortuyn List – already in the 1990s, which has since been succeeded by the Party for Freedom (Partij voor de Vrijheid, PVV) led by Geert Wilders. In Belgium, the Flemish Party Vlaams Belang (formerly Vlaams Blok), the Freedom Party of Austria (Freiheitliche Partei Österreichs, FPÖ) and the Swiss People's Party (Schweizerische Volkspartei, SVP) have all been profiled as nationalist and anti-Islamic movements. Despite the differences between countries, the Danish People's Party (Dansk Folkeparti, DF), Sweden Democrats (Sverigedemokraterna, SD), Norwegian Progress Party (Fremskrittpartiet, FrP) and the Finns Party (Perussuomalaiset, PS) contain similar values and views to the extent that they are placed within a broad grouping of European populist radical right parties (Jungar & Jupskås 2014).

The frontline of nationalist right-wing populism has long been represented in Europe by the National Rally (Rassemblement National, until 2018 Front National, FN) in France and Lega (formerly Lega Nord) in Italy. The National Rally was founded in the early 1970s and was headed by Jean-Marie Le Pen, who led the party until 2011. From the outset, the party has emphasised the national interest and sovereignty of France rather than confederations like the European Union. After Jean-Marie's daughter, Marine Le Pen, took over the leadership of the party, nationalism and anti-Islamic ideas have become increasingly central to party policy. In contrast, Lega has been driven by calls for the independence of the region of Padania, much like the Catalan or Flemish independence movements have done in Spain and Belgium, respectively. However, conservative perspectives on gender roles, religion, anti-immigration and criticism of the EU have played a major role in the Lega's policies and connect it to European right-wing populism. In particular, since Matteo Salvini assumed party leadership in 2013, Lega has shifted from being a northern independence movement to becoming a nationalist right-wing populist party.

The most dominant positions of power attained by right-wing populist movements in Europe have been gained in the East, especially Hungary and Poland. Hungary is dominated by Fidesz – the Hungarian Civic Alliance – and Prime Minister Viktor Orbán, whose leadership has taken the country in an authoritarian direction during the 2010s. In the 2010 elections, the party achieved a landslide victory and an overwhelming majority in parliament, which enabled Fidesz to change the constitution and laws regarding the media. Fidesz held on to its majority in the 2018 elections and has continued its concentration of power also during the COVID-19 pandemic in 2020. The changes have enabled the party to take control of the country's judiciary and have restricted media activities, which have since been kept on a tight leash by those in power. In Poland, the nationalist conservative Law and Justice (Prawo i Sprawiedliwosc, PiS) Party gained a majority in the 2015 parliamentary elections and has tried to follow Fidesz by limiting the activities of the judiciary and the media; however, the party's position has not been written in stone in the same way as Fidesz has managed in Hungary. In Poland, the opposition has been stronger, and Law and Justice has had to take into account the public's protests against the party's authoritarian bent. However, Poland's liberal opposition is as worried as its counterparts are in Hungary.

The strong rise of nationalist political movements in Europe and the United States has linked populism to nationalism and xenophobia to such a degree that the term "populism" has, in many places, become synonymous with extremist nationalism and racism (Brown & Mondon 2020). The fear of strengthening authoritarian regimes has also organically linked populism to fascism and neo-Nazism, or in other words the far right (e.g. Müller 2016; Mudde 2019). This is understandable for historical reasons, but it is also quite problematic because populism is also spoken of in connection with many non-extremist and xenophobic political movements. For example, the left-wing Podemos in Spain and Syriza (The Coalition of the Radical Left) in Greece are European political parties of this millennium that are strongly associated with populism but are in no way to be equated with right-wing nationalist populist parties.

Podemos and Syriza are representatives of left-wing populism, whose core goals have been to defend the nation's economic interests in relation to supranational business corporations, economic unions and organisations. Furthermore, Argentina's Kircherism or Hugo

Chávez's populism in Venezuela has been an integral part of political history and leftist politics in South America. In these contexts, the question of ethnicity has hardly been relevant. One possibility to take into consideration when discussing the multiple forms of populism is precisely the fact that academics and journalists differentiate types of populism by attaching a variety of prefixes and adjectives to the form of populism under discussion. For example, research uses the term "radical right-wing populism" when referring to extremist national and xenophobic populist movements (e.g. Mudde 2007), while in the context of Podemos and Syriza, we speak of "left-wing populism".

Such amendments to the term populism clarify the form being discussed and, depending on the context, are quite useful, but they do not eliminate the ambiguity of populism. Hence, there are a variety of right-wing and left-wing populisms. For example, the Italian comedian's Giuseppe Piero "Beppe" Grillo's Five Star Movement (Movimento 5 Stelle) was in the beginning difficult to classify as either left-wing or right-wing populism, although it was an undeniable populist. Nor can the populist movements that have arisen in different countries in Asia be unproblematically categorised as right or left according to a European model. This is because Asian political systems and cultures differ so much that populism has its own forms in Asia. For example, in connection with East Asia and the Middle East, there has been talk of a "new Islamic populism" that is different from Islamic fundamentalism and which mostly appeals to the disappointed urban middle-class and proletariat in Muslim-majority countries (Hadiz 2016). In South Africa, on the other hand, populism has been linked to the growth pains of young liberal democracy (Vincent 2011). In general, the populist political style is not bound to a division between left and right.

In many political cultures, populism simply means a political style in which voters are wooed with empty promises and provocative language. Populism is, in this sense, a negative term that is also used as a pejorative (Canovan 2005; Bale et al. 2011). When a politician in a multi-party democracy wants to say a competitor lacks ability, they call their opponent populist. In its broadest sense, populism can be linked to any area of life outside of politics, and accusations of populism are found in the realms of culture, economics or sport (see McGuigan 1992). In the same way, the media may use the words populism or populist without careful consideration when it wishes to infer nationalist sycophantic political language for which there is no actual currently appropriate term.

Using populism as a general pejorative or as an umbrella concept that functions as an aid for dealing with a political phenomenon can sometimes be appropriate. However, as a rule, it is loose thinking and a use of language that is more likely to confuse than increase our understanding of politics (Dean & Maiguashca 2020). Speaking of populism, instead of racism, fascism, xenophobia, conservatism, nationalism, nativism, socialism, or any other more specific term, obscures the matter to be dealt with and dulls potentially incisive criticism. Naming a movement populist or accusing a politician of populism can act as a watchword regarding political rhetoric but it does not reveal what makes the speech populist. Instead of the vagueness of populism, it is advisable to use precise expressions, if they exist. Populism is not the same as racism or nationalism, although they are often associated.

In reality, populism began to be considered in political research in the 1950s and 1960s, and the first scholarly books on the subject are from that period (e.g. Shils 1956; Ionescu & Gellner 1969). Actual academic textbooks or monographs on populism began to appear in the 1980s in English and Spanish because populism was specifically associated with North and Latin American political culture (e.g. Canovan 1981; De Ipola 1983). In the American context, populism at that time was largely treated as a phenomenon of agrarian society. Towards the end of the 20th century, a new populism or neo-populism began to be spoken of, especially in many European democracies when nationalist right-wing popular movements began to emerge. The "new wave" of Western populism spawned research and also academic textbooks at the turn of the millennium (e.g. Taggart 2000). The 21st century saw a rise in European research into populism with the publication of key research books on issues such as populism and the media (Mazzoleni et al. 2003), populism and democracy (Mény & Surel 2002; Panizza 2005; Albertazzi & McDonnell 2008), and the relationship between populism and right-wing radicalism (Mudde 2007). In 2005, Ernesto Laclau (1935–2014), a political philosopher from an Argentinian background, published *On Populist Reason* in which he crystallised and drew conclusions on the ideas that he had previously developed together with his colleague Chantal Mouffe. Laclau's thoughts have since sparked fierce debate and strongly divided the field of populism research.

Recently, the study of populism has exploded in the English-speaking world, especially in the 2010s, which is reflected in a major increase in research publications on the issue (Brown & Mondon 2020). This is partly explained by the success of Trump and the vote for Brexit, but also by the continued popularity of the above-mentioned populist movements around the world as well as the stabilisation of populism as a subject of research at European and American universities. Thus, research data on populism is constantly accumulating. The increasing permanence of populist parties within many Western democracies has led to the production of research literature on the subject (e.g. Albertazzi & McDonnell 2015; Akkerman et al. 2016; Eatwell & Goodwin 2018; Norris & Inglehart 2019; Pappas 2019) as has populism's relationship with political communication (e.g. Aalberg et al. 2017; Lochocki 2017; Reinemann et al. 2019) or even the relationship between economic recession and populism (Kriesi & Pappas 2015). New academic textbooks have been written on the subject, in which populism is approached as a political style (Moffitt 2016) or as a "thin" ideology based on antagonism between the people and the elite (Mudde & Kaltwasser 2017). The aim of these approaches has been to overcome the challenge of the multiple faces of populism and to find a perspective that could, like Laclau, parse out a variety of forms of populism. Some textbooks have turned their focus from populism to more ideological underpinnings of radical right and other contemporary political actors challenging democratic institutions (Mudde 2019; Moffitt 2020). In addition to the above, a number of academic books have been published in which populism is more closely linked to the nationalist and xenophobic extreme right, which is seen as a terrifying path to fascism or Nazism (e.g. Wodak 2015; Müller 2016). Academic readers have also been published on the subject (e.g. Kaltwasser et al. 2017; de la Torre 2019).

Nowadays populism is being studied or referred to in many different fields of research. However, roughly speaking, political populism research can be divided into two main lines, one of which is situated in politology and the other in the cultural studies tradition. The politology line has been more popular, but the cultural orientation has also its supporters amongst the academy. Of course, the division is not one-dimensional and many studies combine features of both traditions, but it is possible to draw at least a faint line between them. The essential difference in these paradigms is related to how populism is understood as a research subject and thus how it is approached methodologically.

Simplistically, in the politological tradition populism is understood as a phenomenon that can be defined as a distinct empirical research object separated from the political environment. Some form of positivist current is present in the politological approach, in which the main focus is on defining populism and to which the drawing up and empirical testing of hypotheses is related. For example, some political movements are defined as populist, after which their ideological and electorate activities are analysed with the aid of empirical data. This is why this populism approach is nowadays often called "ideational approach" (Mudde 2017). In politology, the research methods are the tools that make the material more comprehensible. Thus, quantitative methods, such as surveys, content specifications and variance and regression analysis, are popular in the politological approach to populism.

The cultural perspective approaches populism from a constructivist point of view, in which the construction of populism itself is the subject of research. Cultural theorist and art researcher Mieke Bal (2002, 4–5, 9) emphasises the fact that in cultural analysis, concepts are more important than methods. According to Bal (2002, 44), the subjects of analysis are cultural processes and the analysis emphasises intersubjective relations and concepts – while politological empiricism may emphasise clearly defined research subjects (objects), their objective measurement by some method and the evaluation of the research results by a predetermined theory. Thus, the cultural perspective emphasises a qualitative approach to populism. It regards populism as a cultural construction and, according to the approach, it is this very process of construction that should be the subject of research rather than a predefined and empirically measurable populism. Because no pre-defined populist subject can be identified in this approach but populism is seen constructed in contingent political activity, the approach is also called "post-foundationalism" (Marchart 2007).

This book applies the cultural approach in defining populism, because I believe it essentially captures the emotional experiences and courses of action taken in relation to the emergence and construction of populism. However, the book is not fully committed to constructivism or the "post-foundationalist" idea of changes in the political environment preventing the restoration of basic principles, such as ideologies and parties, to politics. In my view, party politics and the political system have a strong position in democracies and also in people's lives; thus, there is no reason to abandon the discussion of populism as it is related to both democracy and party politics as highly influential empirical phenomena. Politological research has produced a wealth of empirical research on topics identified as belonging to populism and has developed a high volume of cumulative knowledge about the phenomenon, which can be seen for example in this book in the chapters on the relationship between populism and democracy as well as populism and the media.

Therefore, this book differs from other works of populism in that it tries to build a bridge between politological or ideational populism research and cultural approach that often are seen as contradictory.

In this context, populism is not limited to the examination of individual political movements and politicians; instead, I approach populism as a general political phenomenon using both theoretical and historical perspectives. Empirical research related to populist movements serves, of course, as one source of material for the book, and I have myself also thoroughly studied the relationship between populist parties and the media in the Northern European context.

Nevertheless, the main purpose of the book is to open up populism as a general and local political phenomenon from a variety of perspectives. In this, the cultural approach serves an interesting starting point, because it emphasis the significance of contexts in populist constellations. Therefore, the cultural approach is here applied, especially in understanding and defining what is at stake in populism, but politological research is used to open up the consequences of populism in political life, party politics and democracies on a more concrete level. *A cultural approach to populism means here that populism is understood as an affective identification and signification process in which a political identity is constructed through the use of various ideologically or morally laden cultural symbols and markers of the people and their alleged enemies.* Thus, political party structures or electorates are seen as consequences of populism, which is understood culturally as a meaning-making process for political identities.

Populism as a term and phenomenon arouses emotions. Additionally, populism research stimulates the minds because it often takes a stand on whether a political phenomenon is good or bad. Especially many politological studies of populism have a normative current in which populism is criticised. This is understandable, particularly when the form of populism is based on the exclusion of some groups in society and often emphasises hostility towards them – because they are defined as being different from the "people", for example, due to ethnicity. Populism is connected, with good reason, to authoritarian political tendencies, most recently demonstrated in riots linked to Donald Trump's loss in the US 2020 presidential elections. Populism has been negatively charged as a word, and that negativity is reflected in academic language too (Bale et al. 2011). In this phrasing, populists are evil and populism is seen as a threat that must be overcome. I too have a negative attitude towards populism as a force and method that viciously ostracises one section of society at the expense of another, but in this book, populism is not approached in a normative way. Populism can be associated with a wide range of political phenomena and analytically taken it is also possible to see it sometimes in a positive light. This book will shed light on these different aspects of populism.

In this book, populism is specifically dealt with in political frameworks and, even if applying a cultural approach, so-called "cultural populism" is only addressed when it is linked to politics (cf. McGuigan 1992). The aim of the book is to clarify the debate and discussion on populism and the use of the term populism in different contexts. The work is based on both the author's own research and that of others. The next chapter of the book specifically opens up the theoretical discussion on populism and explains how the phenomenon has been defined in academic research. At the end of the chapter, I present my own definition of populism based a separate synthesis of earlier definitions.

The second chapter of the book succinctly presents an overview of populism's various historical forms as structured in research. The historical review is important in that it helps to place modern populist currents in the continuum of politics and simultaneously contextualising our understanding of what is occurring in politics in the present day. Although populism is also associated with authoritarian regimes, in this work the interest is primarily on populism as part of democratic systems. The third chapter therefore focuses on the special relationship between populism and democracy. The popularity of populism in the United States, Western Europe and the Nordic countries makes the consideration of the issue especially topical – after all, these regions are regarded as amongst the strongest bastions of liberal democracy.

The fourth chapter deepens the relationship between populism and the media. According to many researchers, the role of the media plays an integral role in the strengthening and spread of the populist spirit. At the same time, the liberal news media is perplexed by populist provocations. The increased role of social media in political communication makes the current situation particularly interesting. The fifth chapter examines populism in relation to three frameworks or concepts, which I use to broaden the context in which modern populism has gained popularity. These concepts are the welfare state, globalisation and postmodernism. Of these, postmodernism is the most controversial and perhaps nebulous concept in social science literature. In my view, however, postmodern debate suits populism very well and quite aptly describes some of its essential features, such as the central importance of identity politics, emotionalism and nostalgia's centrality in populism, and therefore links populism inherently to cultural approach. It is no coincidence that postmodern theories flourished at the same time as the new wave of European populism began to gain in popularity in the 1980s and 1990s. The book ends with reflections on the importance of populism in political life in the near future especially in regard to the COVID-19 pandemic and Donald Trump's fall from the US presidency in 2020.

Empirical populism research has largely focused on European, North American and Latin American populism, although a number of studies have recently been published on Asian and African populism, demonstrating its ubiquitousness (e.g. Thompson 2010; Vincent 2011; Rodan 2012; Hadiz & Robinson 2017). A general feature of populism research regarding these parts of the world is that it sees the rise of populism by explaining it as a reaction to the neoliberal ideological emphasis on globalisation, which has produced major structural changes in national economies and labour markets (Hadiz & Chryssogelos 2017). In addition, the analyses demonstrate that the thin and short history of democratic systems in those countries almost invariably leads to populism being used to install an authoritarian power. Thus, although the focus is on the author's research interests in European and American populism, populism is dealt with on such a general level that the ideas contained in this book are in many ways applicable to other contexts of populism.

Populism has been around for as long as there has been modern politics and populism will remain as long as politics is the way people organise their social lives. However, it may well be argued that in politics in the 21st century we are living in an age of a particular type of populism as political movements – to a large extent around the world (Hadiz & Chryssogelos 2017) – are riding on a similar type of populist logic that has emerged. By emphasising individuality and affective experiences, politics and the hybrid media environment have created an excellent framework by which populists' identifications can rise and form political groupings. However, the COVID-19 pandemic and Donald Trump's defeat brought new kinds of challenges to the two-decade triumph of populism in 2020. Therefore, it is very timely to look at what academic research has to say about populism as a simultaneously global and local political phenomenon.

1 What is populism?

A number of academic scholars met in the mid-1960s at the London School of Economics to discuss the problem of populism (see Ionescu & Gellner 1969). Their aim was to define populism as a phenomenon, but the result was somewhat confusing due to translation problems and a collection of fragmented perspectives on populism as an ideology and movement. The same confusion has continued to exist amongst researchers in the 21st century due to the fact that populism is associated with so many diverse types of political phenomena and movements; thus, an unambiguous definition is difficult to make. Hence, populism theorists have repeatedly complained about the difficulty of defining populism, leading to it being called chameleon-like (Taggart 2000). It has also been considered a vague or obscure concept and consequently many political researchers have not wanted to use the term (see Canovan 1999). Some have even come to believe that populism is an unanalytical concept that it is not useful for research, and justifiable warnings about using the term vaguely have arisen (Dean & Maiguashca 2020; Goyvaerts & De Cleen 2020).

Nevertheless, the study of populism continues to expand. The strengthening of nationalist and anti-immigration movements in the 21st century led to the avalanche of right-wing populism, while Brexit and the election of Trump as the President of the United States in 2016 placed populism as a subject squarely in the Anglo-American research community. Research methods and subjects respond to changes in society – and currently there is a growth in and a qualified need for research into populism. Alongside this rise in research, there has been an increase in the academic understanding of populism and a burgeoning of data. Furthermore, the need to define populism seems more pressing today than it was at the end of the 1960s, when the modern base for the academic study of political populism was established. The 1960s were still experiencing the intense industrialisation and

DOI: 10.4324/9781003267539-2

urbanisation that were established after the Second World War, leading to structural changes that revolutionised political life and created the opportunity for the welfare state and so-called agrarian populism. Consequently, populism was defined and approached as a political phenomenon that resulted from the reaction to the disintegration of rural communities and the increased fragmentation of life in urban environments.

Perhaps the most widely used definition of political populism in research today is based on Cas Mudde's work. According to Mudde (2004, 543), "Populism is an ideology that considers society to be ultimately separated into two homogenous and antagonistic groups: 'the pure people' and 'the corrupt elite', and argues that politics should be an expression of the *volonté générale* (general will) of the people". Mudde has since slightly modified the definition by complementing the ideological description and now speaks of a "thin-centred ideology", a phrase inspired by Michael Freeden (1996), but otherwise the definition has remained almost the same (Mudde 2007, 23; Mudde & Kaltwasser 2012a, 8). The thin-centred ideology modification was derived from a lively debate in which the defining of populism as a clear ideology has been criticised. However, this definition and "ideational approach" on populism have been perhaps the most popular orientations in contemporary populism studies.

Mudde's formulation is seen as a "minimal definition of populism", and it therefore raises most of the recurring themes of populism and highlights them: the concept of the people, the forming of a group, the confrontation and antagonism between different groups, the ideology behind those confrontations and the perspective of the role of populism in politics. I will next examine in more detail those definitions of populism that have emphasised certain aspects of the above-mentioned individual themes as the main denominators of populism. The aim is to open the background to the theoretical debate of populism. At the end of the chapter, I present a slightly modified version of a definition of populism, which, in particular, echoes Ernesto Laclau's cultural understanding of populism in addition to the Muddean approach.

Appealing to the people

In everyday language, populism often means the wooing or the agitating (demagogy) of the people, often by methods that are termed cheap talk or opportunistic (see Taguieff 2002). The concept of the people is at the heart of the definition of populism, stemming from the fact that the word populism comes from the Latin word "populus" that means the people. How the notion of the people is understood varies from one person to another. This is because "the people" is itself about as vague a concept as populism (Canovan 2005, 2). Acting in the name of the people has occurred since time began – and depending on the era and context – completely different policies have been enacted. Consequently, "the people" have been harnessed as a tool for a huge variety of diverse political aims (Koselleck 1989).

It can be categorically stated that an unambiguous group that can be called "the people" does not actually exist anywhere. The people always consist of individuals, some of whom, according to different definitions, are "more people" than others. For example, in the city of Athens, half a century before the Common Era, fully fledged citizens could only be free men. Women, children, slaves and metics did not belong to the people; they were not citizens. Benedict Anderson (1983), a scholar of historical nationalism, presented the idea that nations are imaginary communities. When small communities were transferred into nation states, the nations had to be consciously built. That construction of nation required language, stories, communication of information, literature, culture and common symbols (Hobsbawm & Ranger 1983). Thus, the people can be considered a fiction that must be specifically invented (Morgan 1988).

Nonetheless, the belief in a united people as a nation and a pillar of democracy is strong. Without such faith, nations would not exist; thus, the imagined community is not merely fiction or myth; it has concrete consequences. In the name of shared communality, nations organise themselves into societies; they organise the interaction and human life. Without the imagined communality, there would be no countries cooperating in the international community with other states. Imagined and created communities also compete against each other on the sports fields and economically, even at times going to war. The people may have been imagined but the concept also becomes an actor – in the people's name and working against it (Canovan 2005).

The concept of the people has been used in many struggles during political history. The people were certainly an important concept when the idea of a unified nation state was introduced at the beginning of the 19th century. The people were also a key term when civil society and its internal national divisions were structured later in European and American contexts. The concept of the people plays a central role in the definition of a unified nation and in the struggles concerning its internal structures (Koselleck 1989). The use of the term "the people" based on an ethnic, linguistic and cultural distinctiveness is therefore only one form of nationalism; thus, returning "the people" to this sort of exclusionary nationalism does not necessarily do justice to the concept.

Thus, nationalism or patriotism can be seen as a positive phenomenon because their lack would mean it is not possible to build the nation states that have proved to be historically well-functioning units of social organisation. At its best, nationalism acts specifically as an idea that unites different groups of people, creating opportunities for organising co-existence despite differences. However, the reverse side of nationalism is the exclusionary nationalism that only accepts certain groups of people as "the people" and treats others as enemies. This becomes nativism and is precisely the ideology in which "the native citizens" of a country are considered the source of the nation, while people representing languages and cultures from elsewhere are seen as a threat (Mudde 2007, 19). That form of extremist nationalism can also be associated with populist movements; hence, in this book I usually refer to exclusionary nationalism when I use the term nationalism in the context of right-wing populist political parties.

In democracies, the idea of the sovereignty of the people has been central. It is this that distinguishes democracy from other more central forms of government where people are not citizens but subjects. The word "democracy" (demos-kratos) ultimately means the people decide. In reality, of course, this is not true. There are so many different types of people living in nation states that the issues facing a nation can never be decided on unanimously. In representative democracies, this issue has been resolved by the people periodically casting votes in elections to elect decision makers who represent the interests of the people.

"The people" has had a special meaning in populism because the idea of common people and the expression of their will is the starting point of populism, consequently citing the term "the people" is used as an ultimate justification (Canovan 2005, 80). In fact, populism generally comes from disappointment with representative democracy or the functioning of democracy. When populism rises, it is commonly believed that the rank and file of the people have been forgotten by politicians, that so-called ordinary people no longer have a voice in politics. Peter Wiles (1969, 166) summarised this concept in his early contribution within populism by stating that "virtue resides in the simple people, who are the overwhelming majority, and in their collective traditions".

Hence, populism is often justified by the fact that it concerns a part of the nation that has been forgotten and which, it is claimed, represents the majority. In other words, according to populists, representative democracy does not work because a minority makes decisions without listening to the majority. This claim contains seeds of truth as, in many representative democracies, voting power has fallen at the same time as participation in party politics interests fewer people (Manin 1997). Outside of those citizens who are politically active, there are people for whom politics holds no interest because they feel that they cannot influence it or are excluded from political life. Some of this group eagerly grasp the populist promise that democracy will be restored to their hands.

Nevertheless, an essential part of populism is that not all the citizens of a nation represent the people. It may also be that what populists call "the people" is a very small part of the nation, even a minority. For example, in Western multi-party democracies, populist parties have, at best, received roughly 20 per cent of the votes cast in parliamentary elections while support for their movements is no higher than opinion polls show. It is true that on some individual issues, populist movements may even represent the opinion of the majority of the people, but in most cases this is not the case, and quite often the majority of citizens do not want to give populists a mandate to promote issues by using the power of the majority. During this millennium in Europe, Hungary is the closest to an exception in this respect, resulting in a shift to an authoritarian use of power. In Turkey and Russia, presidential powers have also reached a position in the 2010s where they can rely on a simple majority without referring to the consent of the minority, but to what extent this is actually populism is another question.

In addition, it is possible to ask whether the will of the people can be trusted or measured in any sensible way. Even if majority vote is an essential measure in representative democracies, all voting methods are problematic regarding the expression of the will of a majority: the voting method produces an election result but does not provide any guarantee of the functionality of decisions made for the majority (Gaertner 2006; Hindmoor 2006). For this reason, opinion polls and referendums do not, therefore, act as the will of the people. These are necessary reminders of the limitations of the concept of "the people" and the will of the majority as a justification for policy.

Appealing to the people is an understandable starting point for populists because the concept of the people is so central to populism – they seek power from the "people", and a group will call for the right to define the people from its own essence. It may, however, be argued that politics is, in general, a public provocation and that all politicians appeal to the people – at least during election campaigns when trying to attract as many voters as possible. There is no policy without an appeal to the people and for that reason, a more specific approach to the problem of populism has been sought, for example, through the concept of ideology.

Ideology

The concept of ideology is not much more unambiguous than populism or the people. In a broad sense, ideology is the system of ideas and beliefs that govern human behaviour. For example, in Marxist theory, ideology means the ability of the capitalist system to produce social structures, institutions and practices that enable capitalism to reproduce and justify itself from one decade to the next. In the field of cultural studies, however, ideology is often identified with common beliefs, the so-called common sense, by which people structure the world in well-trodden and reproducible ways (e.g. Hall 1988). This also sits well with the populist worldview, which is believed to be the people's intuitive and experiential view of the world of expenditure. According to the French Marxist philosopher Louis Althusser (1918–1990), ideology calls us as subjects; in other words, capitalist culture is interpellated with our identities through ideology (Althusser 1971). In a broader sense, the idea also explains why everyday reason or common sense feels like a natural way to understand the world: it has permeated us to become part of our identities. The grip of ideology is based on the fact that it makes itself become such a natural and invisible part of the self (Glynos & Howarth 2007, 117).

However, in political sciences, ideology is generally regarded as a more restrictive system, which guides the action of people (e.g. Freeden 1996; Moffitt 2020). In politics, dominant ideologies have been separated, such as Marxist-based socialism, individual and economic freedom emphasising liberalism, as well as conservatism that accentuates traditional values.

Conservatism emerged at the end of the 18th century as a counterreaction to the spread of enlightenment ideals and revolutionary activity in order to defend continuity and older systems of power; thus, it can be considered a reactionary ideology. Liberalism and socialism are, in turn, reformist or radical ideologies that represent the power of change. Today, conservatism is also often associated with nationalism, which can also be considered an ideology. At the time of the construction of national states, nationalism was clearly a radical ideology challenging the order of previous eras (Anderson 1983). Traditionally, in modern politics, conservatism and nationalism are linked to the right and liberalism and socialism to the left. Thus, economic and value-liberalism do not necessarily go hand in hand, especially in today's world, where these divisions are often confused: the economic right may represent liberal values, for example, with regard to sexual minorities and immigrants, while on the left, the national economic interest can be emphasised in the name of the majority and at the expense of minorities.

Donald MacRae (1969, 154) was of the opinion in the late 1960s that populism should be treated as an ideology, even though the concept of ideology in sociological and political analysis was quite controversial at that time. Of the known ideologies, populism is particularly associated with conservatism and nationalism. Above all, this is true for right-wing populism, where nationalism and the defence of traditional values – home, religion, patriotism – have played a key role. On the other hand, the political movements listed as populist and identified at the beginning of this book show that populism has been associated with so many different ideologies that it is very difficult to find any solid ideological background into which all the world's populists could be placed. Unlike, for example, the political left or right around the world, populism does not have a common system of doctrine, catechism or reference on which political action can be built. Additionally, significant populist characters are also usually national rather than international (Stanley 2008; Aslanidis 2016).

It is clear that populism is not ideology in the same sense as capitalism, socialism, liberalism, conservatism or nationalism, but that does not mean that populism does not have anything to do with ideology. For example, MacRae (1969) saw populism as a central ideology of primitivism, in which a non-intellectualism in the form of the pursuit of some sort of naturalism as well as romantic and conservative utopianism was present – a hankering for a previous era and way of life. MacRae's vision of the ideology of populism stems from the time of agrarian populism, which was a reaction to the strong industrialisation and the hollowing out of rural communities when people moved to cities. However, this view also resonates with today's populism, which often has the idea of a former genuine golden era in which a nation was unified and happy – when the will of the people was realised. Paul Taggart (2000), for example, has called the longing for such a "heartland" a core idea of populism.

Current populism is often characterised by a strong nostalgia for the past. As such, contemporary populism can be considered a typical postmodern phenomenon (Jameson 1991). Although populists themselves often rely on traditional values and stability, their entire existence denies the postmodern production of uncertainty in human life. While the modern era has brought order and certainty to people's lives, postmodernism has challenged established family forms, employment and occupations, working life, nationalities and nation states in the 21st century in a way that causes anxiety and uncertainty about the future. Hankering for the past is a drug for combating uncertainty. Populism is, in this sense, a counter-reaction to postmodern ideology, which can also be seen in populist cultural policy favouring the nationalist and romantic epoch at the cost of contemporary postmodern pluralism.

However, in the different populisms that exist, nostalgia for the past varies. Nostalgia is most often associated with right-wing populism in which nationalism plays a significant role. In contrast, nostalgia for a perceived utopia or conservative primitivism has a much smaller significance for left-wing populism. In fact, in the populism of Beppe Grillo or similar direct democracy proponents, such nostalgic longing usually plays no role.

Researchers have begun to call populism a thin ideology because it is clearly related to ideologies but does not represent any single system of ideas or a fully rounded ideology (Moffitt 2020). Ben Stanley (2008, 107), for example, sees the ideological thinness of populism as its strength: "in practice it is a complementary ideology: it does not so much overlap with as diffuse itself throughout full ideologies". This chameleon quality of populism, the ability to use different ideologies according to the demands of the situation, helps to explain populism's influence and its connections to very different political movements and perspectives. However, the fact that populism is not a full or whole ideology does not make it non-political or free of ideologies.

In political sciences, the most used definition of populism relies on the ideational approach and Mudde's description of populism as "thin-centred ideology" (Mudde 2017, 27–30). The ideational approach combines different studies that view populism as a "set of ideas" that construct a strong antagonism between pure and good people and a corrupt and evil elite. According to the ideational approach, populism also stands in opposition to pluralism by emphasising the unity of the majority. Scholars included in the ideational approach might also have called populism discourse or style, but basically they treat it similarly as a set of ideas constructing antagonisms in the political life (Hawkins & Kaltwasser 2017, 514–516). However, the main focus in the ideational approach has been on empirical analyses and, as far as I can see, it leaves the relationship between populism and ideology still rather unclear. Cultural theory can clarify this relationship perhaps better.

In the 1970s, Ernesto Laclau presented the articulation theory that explained the multiplicity of the ideological forms of populism. Laclau (1977) was critical of the Orthodox Marxist theory that class structures explain the origins of and differences between political movements. Laclau, who was involved in the left-wing movement of the time, found that political representation did not conform to class structures but was more a question of cultural identity and influences. In particular, he applied the concept of hegemony developed by the Italian Marxist theorist, Antonio Gramsci (1891–1937), according to which power is maintained in society by persuasion and constant negotiation rather than by class structures that were cut in stone. The attainment of hegemonic power requires the approval of repressed citizens, which can only be achieved by invoking culturally common values, morals and ideologies (Gramsci 2011 [1947]).

According to the articulation theory, social classes do not necessarily correspond to real groups of people because classes are ultimately derived from interpretations of class structures, which also use different cultural meanings that are unrelated to class structures. This explains why different ideologies and cultural meanings can be articulated or connected as needed, so that the populism of the time can respond to the political needs of the group whose support it seeks. For example, in right-wing populism, nationalism, xenophobia and conservatism will strike a chord that is heard across class structures. At a time when globalisation and technological development from major structural changes in industry and when people's mobility has increased along with the spread of liberal values, such articulation becomes understandable. In populism, the concept of a forgotten people is of great importance, but those people are not tied to a single social class (Laclau 1977, 160–166). Supporters of current populist movements represent people from different socio-economic backgrounds. For example, Western right-wing populist parties do have certain demographic features, such as male domination, vocational backgrounds and individuals feeling that they are threatened by unemployment, but socio-economically their voters are often rather average wage earners and are heterogeneous.

According to Laclau (1977, 167), the significance of cultural articulation is that very different political movements can use the same ideologically charged symbols when appealing to their supporters. National symbols such as flags and coats of arms are typical examples of symbols harnessed to the use of various populist and other political actors. Internationally, an even more striking example is the face of Che Guevara (1928–1967), an Argentinian-born Marxist revolutionary, whose image has spread via t-shirts and coffee cups and the strangest of connections. When Che Guevara was striving for a communist revolution in Cuba, Congo and Bolivia in the 1950s and 1960s, he could hardly anticipated how much wealth capitalists would have made by using his image to sell products and how different types of "young rebels" – rockers, nerds, hipsters, start-up entrepreneurs – can combine his image with their own dreams. In these articulations, Che Guevara means general rebellion and revolutionary practices regardless of ideology.

Articulation theory also explains why populism is a thin rather than a solid ideology and it also explains why different types of ideologies can randomly unite in populism in very unexpected ways. As the cultural scholar Stuart Hall (1932–2014) reminds us, the gaze must be directed to the context if one is to understand the emergence of political articulation. The breaking of a hegemonic power block usually creates space for populism, which responds to the calls of the people in a power vacuum. According to Hall (1988), this was behind the rise of Margaret Thatcher (1925–2013) in Britain in the late 1970s as left-wing power had lost credibility. This has also happened in many European liberal democracies of this millennium, where right-wing populist movements have broken the hegemonic power of social democratic movements and have caused the left to lose elections. At the same time, right-wing populists have succeeded in attracting national conservative voters also from the central right (Lochocki 2017). Populism can perhaps outwardly appear as a political style that is appealing to the people, but by analysing the political environment of the time, one can also understand the ideological background behind the emergence of populism.

Political style

The endless debate about whether or not populism is an ideology has led some scholars to reduce populism to a political style. In their opinion, populism is not about anything other than the rhetoric or the style in which issues are presented. This view makes sense in that it can explain very different phenomena associated with populism. If populism is understood as a pure style, every politician can be a populist if necessary. The definition is supported in particular in Anglo-American political culture, where rhetoric and acting skills have long been at the heart of political communication. The definition also explains the loading of populism with negative meanings. Accusing someone of being a populist – based on their language and political culture – has been a typical way to attack or criticise political rivals in Western democracies (Bale et al. 2011).

Research into the use of the word "populism" in Western countries has revealed that the most common meaning of the term in political speech is that it refers to empty rhetoric, the making of unconditional promises or the attacking and criticising of political rivals (Canovan 2005; Bale et al. 2011; Herkman 2016). Some media and communications researchers also point out that the populist style is deliberately used in politics to attract attention. Populist politicians are deliberately provocative, presenting polarising political views and generating confrontation, which creates media publicity and forces the creation of a desired political agenda (Mazzoleni 2008; Wodak 2015; Moffitt 2016). The supporters of right-wing populists are not afraid of negative media publicity because they agree on issues and bundle the mainstream news media into an enemy camp, accusing the media of being part of the liberal elite. Populists also often emphasise that they speak on difficult issues in the language of ordinary people. According to them, politicians in power talk around subjects and do not say what they think, using formal language and civil servant speech. Thus, a positive starting point for populism emphasises speaking in a style that ordinary people understand.

Since populism cannot be defined as a unified ideology in the same way as, for example, socialism or liberalism can, some scholars believe it is unnecessary to speak of a thin ideology. For example, Paris Aslanidis (2016) sets aside the idea of Mudde's definition of populism and defines a discursive frame of populism. In discursive framing, our understanding of the world is framed or enclosed or made meaningful. Thus, with reference to populism, it is a way of expressing and structuring things, such as building a confrontation between forgotten people and an elite or immigrants. According to Aslanidis, populism is discourse and not ideology.

Benjamin Moffitt (2016) understands populism in a somewhat similar way but with a stronger emphasis on the concept as a political style or media performance. The general notion is that politics in general has begun to emphasise performance skills, visible habits, private life and public performance due to the requirements of media publicity (Manin 1997; Stanyer 2007). This US-style political presence has also spread to Europe, and the European media have moved closer to the American liberal model (Hallin & Mancini 2004). Politics can be said to have become mediatised, meaning that the influence of all media is believed to have increased in politics (e.g. Esser & Strömbäck 2014). According to some researchers, we live in audience democracies, where citizens mainly follow the performance of politics in the media (Manin 1997; Meyer 2002). In such an environment, the populist style, which makes direct appeals to the people, has a brash and abrasive style and creates scandal, jutting out like a nail on a barn wall.

There are different definitions of populist style as part of political communication; however, the connecting features are generally regarded as the concept of appealing to the people and opposing elites and members of society who are not regarded as belonging to the people (Jagers & Walgrave 2007; Reinemann et al. 2017). Style can be used in media presentations as well as in social media updates and is not linked to any particular political group or actor. Thus, if necessary, a populist style can be used by all political actors.

Often, it is the humour used by populists that distinguishes populism from serious, dull and technocratic official language. Many populists are known from their humorous quips. For example, the leader of the UKIP party, Nigel Farage, became known for his abrasive humour and anti-EU insults, some of which even generated international condemnation, as they often targeted people like Herman van Rompuy, who was President of the European Council from 2009 to 2014. On the other hand, populists often justify their insults as "just a joke" but use them to cement group identifications (see Billig 2001). Expressing coarse opinions is also typical within populist circles, but the public face of populist movements will outwardly express more moderate opinions, while those not in the public eye will use coarse and vulgar language.

Understanding populism as a political style helps in empirical research. When populism is defined only by some features of political rhetoric or presentation, it is also easy to quantify and analyse. For example, Jan Jagers and Stefaan Walgrave (2007) have studied party speeches in the early 2000s in Belgium and define populism as a style of political communication. They separated the three elements of style: referencing the people, anti-elitism and the exclusion of those considered others or different. By understanding populism in this way, Jagers and Walgrave were able to build indexes from the three elements that they could quantify by comparing how "populist" the different parties were in their communication. Highest on the index of populist behaviour were anti-elitism and the exclusion of other groups of people, such as immigrants, from the definition of the nation.

However, Jagers and Walgrave (2007, 336–337) found that the reduction of populism to mere style was inadequate. In their definitions, populism was accompanied by a strong confrontation between the "pure people" and elites or others, for example, immigrants. Such confrontation is always ideological. As not all vulgar or provocative political style is populist, understanding populism as purely a political style is problematic in the same way as thinking that the idea of populism is the wooing of the people. In order for the political style to be connected to populism, what is required is a confrontation between the people and other groups. Consequently, populism as a mere political style easily develops into a superficial approach (Mazzoleni 2014). Populism is also very often associated with a political movement, as discussed earlier. Political movements, on the other hand, are unlikely to arise without some sort of ideology or value base on which the movement can be built (Minogue 1969, 204). Discourses – different established habits of language and systems – are organically linked to the structures and material reality of society. Political language always gains meaning in some context.

It is therefore important to distinguish a clear line between ideology and the ideological, the latter referring to the use and application of systems of thought for differing moral purposes. Populism is not an ideology, but it is ideological. Populist statements and movements are based on strong moral arguments and those arguments are supported by different ideologies as required. For example, in right-wing populist movements, it is believed that one's own nation is the most important, and benefitting it must be placed above all else. The background to this is the nationalistic ideology of the importance of the nation or the nativist ideology of native citizens threatened by people, languages and cultures from elsewhere (Mudde 2007). The result is a policy that tightens border controls, immigration and customs, and reduces social benefits for minorities. In left-wing movements, however, it is believed that supranational business and corporations threaten the sovereignty of the people. In the background to socialist ideology, there is the belief that a strong state acts as a restraint on the market and business corporations. The result is a policy of trying to bring the economy under political control and opposing intervention from outside the nation.

This is precisely why the ideational approach of populism sees it as a Manichean perspective on the political world, equating good with "the will of the pure people" and evil with a conspiring elite (Hawkins & Kaltwasser 2017; Mudde 2017). However, as Laclau's, Aslanidis', Moffit's and other studies demonstrate, ideology, political style and movement are always closely linked to each other in political populism, and it is very difficult to discern which of them is the most dominating feature in populism. This may also vary depending on context and populist actors.

Political movements

Thus, populism is a question of antagonism, in which the forgotten people are set against other groups, such as the elite or immigrants. Usually, there are strong protest characteristics in populism. Populism is typically a non-movement or an anti-movement that is opposed to something rather than a matter of searching to find new alternatives. Populists are generally opposed to all kinds of (political, economic, cultural) elites, immigration, multiculturalism, tolerance, bureaucracy, technocracy, big money, big companies or the European Union. According to MacRae (1969, 56), due to its protest characteristics, populism produces short-lived social and political movements rather than long-standing and well-organised parties (also Taggart 2000, 99; Canovan 2005, 89).

These findings apply to some populist movements but not to all. It is true that a large number of populist movements ride on antagonisms, which are then used to produce emotions and to attract supporters. However, this does not mean that they would not have their own agenda. In addition to resisting, populist movements invariably also promote some issues. The other side of being anti-immigration is to favour native citizens. Opposing business corporations or the European Union inevitably leads to desiring strong national control over the economy. In turn, the opposition to social elites and corruption is justified by the need for direct democracy and the strengthening of civil society. Thus, there are usually strong moral or ideological underpinnings behind the protest of populist movements.

Populist movements have come and gone and compared to the many political parties of the left, right and centre established in Western-style democracies, these movements have often been short-lived. Many of the current populist right-wing parties have been founded on the foundations of faded populist parties. For example, in 1995, the Danish People's Party rose from the support the Progress Party (Fremskridstpartiet) had lost, and in the same year, the Finns Party was born from the ruins of the Finnish Rural Party (SMP). What is common is that when a populist party comes to power, its support begins to dwindle, because the party cannot keep its promises and its supporters become disillusioned. Some scholars have argued that populism is specifically related to current protest movements that cannot maintain support for long periods because they lack a structured party organisation and an established support community (e.g. Wiles 1969, 168).

However, some researchers point out that many of the current European (right-wing) populist parties are astonishingly long-lived and well-established (e.g. Albertazzi & McDonnell 2008; Zaslove 2008). In Holland, Belgium, Austria, Switzerland, France, Italy and the Nordic countries, there have been influential radical right political parties for 20–40 years. They have made significant progress during elections and been active during several parliamentary terms, even functioning within governments. Many of these parties have consciously built up their party organisations and strengthened their support base by committing people to their organisations. In some European countries, such as Hungary and Poland, radical right parties have gained ruling positions in society at large.

Although populist movements can rise as protest or counter-movements, the background to their political success is always based on genuine political issues. In most cases, populist movements arise when societal crises or epoch-making changes occur. For example, the rise of the Nazi party from a marginal protest movement to a nationally influential political party was strengthened by the great economic recession Germany experienced for which it offered quick-fix solutions (see Hobsbawm 1994). It is the extreme right that is considered to benefit most from economic problems. The international financial crisis, which began in 2008 and expanded into a general economic crisis, particularly in the eurozone, has been reported by some researchers as generating a leap in support for right-wing populists in Europe (e.g. Kriesi & Pappas 2015). In general, however, it is thought that economic crises are less important for populism than some sort of political crisis. For example, many of the radical right parties in central and northern Europe have become popular in the 21st century during economic times that can be considered at least reasonable (see Panizza 2005, 11–12).

A political crisis means that established parties are unable to effectively discuss issues with their citizens or adequately respond to their problems (Laclau 2005). In the Western world, at the end of the 20th century, there was a long period where interest in politics, party engagement and voting declined; a period when political parties resembled each other ideologically, politics became technocratic and people felt unable to influence their lives through traditional party politics (Manin 1997). This created room for populist movements that offered simple solutions and quick opportunities for influence. Populists are skilful at creating crisis thinking and thus feeding their own needs by emphasising that the political system has broken down and then promising to remedy the situation.

The wave of populism that has emerged since the mid-20th century has been regarded as a kind of continuation of late 19th century agrarian populist movements. According to populist theorists, the agrarian movements were a counter-reaction to modernisation and, in particular, the associated industrialisation (Stewart 1969, 185–186). At the turn of this century, right-wing populism is believed to be largely a response to the challenges globalisation poses to nation states (e.g. Panizza 2005). The rise in Asian populism, such as in Indonesia and Thailand, has also been linked to the neoliberal globalisation of the economy, which has radically changed local labour markets (e.g. Hadiz & Chryssogelos 2017).

The ability to control political decision-making or the economy at the national level has been significantly weakened by globalisation (Held & McGrew 2002). The importance of multinationals, trade unions and trading blocs like the European Union has increased and the scope for action available to national decision makers has narrowed. Global markets have produced major structural changes within industries and working lives while simultaneously increasing mobility and migration. If we add to this the military crises in Africa, the Middle East and the Caucasus, which have caused a massive movement of refugees to more prosperous countries, it is no surprise therefore that right-wing populist parties appealing to nationalism have received support in many countries. Populist movements thrive as long as the political environment provides the ground for their success and other parties are unable to adequately respond to the concerns and demands of citizens.

Populism can also be associated with the early stages of political parties. The early history of left-wing opposition and workers' struggles or the initial protests of the green movement were full of emotion-provoking rhetoric, great promises and radical action. Populism is an integral part of the birth pains of a political movement trying to challenge the *status quo* of the political hegemony (Laclau & Mouffe 1985). When a movement becomes established as an organised party, this usually signals a step towards a more moderate and conciliatory culture of action. Furthermore, the success of the parliamentary elections normalises the party, which then has to pay attention to the performances and statements of its members, while government responsibilities further increase such requirements. Typically, populist parties who begin with extremist tendencies lose their most radical members via resignations or by being forced out as their movement stabilises its position in the political arena (cf. Sartori 2005 [1976]). Thus, populist movements normalise and become mainstream when they establish themselves within a political system (Wiles 1969; Akkerman et al. 2016).

Nevertheless, not all movements alter significantly and in many populist parties the idea of defending the mass of the people and confronting elites or immigrants remains the core idea. In many cases, populist actors hold on to at least some of their radicalism even after being successful in national elections (Akkerman et al. 2016). Donald Trump is a good example of a populist leader who amazingly retained his "populist approach" while President of the United States. This has also preserved the faith his support base shows in him. Populist parties may also look for new confrontations to maintain a populist protest spirit and group identity. When a party normalises and becomes a sufficiently mainstream political organisation, its populist identity may disappear due to institutionalisation. In this sense, populism can be seen as one of the characteristics of the development arcs of political parties. On the other hand, in extreme cases, a populist movement can also find itself winning a simple majority, and it then begins to rule a country in an authoritarian manner – examples of that from both Europe and the Americas can be found.

Populism is therefore generally associated with political movements, although it cannot be reduced to a single type of movement. As the examples from the beginning of the book reveal, populism is linked to so many different movements that finding a common denominator between them is difficult if not impossible. In addition, it can be argued that some of the populism is attached to a person rather than a movement. Most populist movements have a strong and distinctive leading figure around which the movement builds. In the Americas, leader-based populism is especially prevalent – Juan and Evita Perón's "Peronist" tradition can be said to have created a template for populism (Taggart 2000) – and Donald Trump has become emblematic of populism in the United States in the 2010s and 2020s. Leader-based populism is also common in Europe, where charismatic politicians like Marine Le Pen, Jörg Haider, Geert Wilders, Nigel Farage, Pia Kjærsgaard, Jimmie Åkesson, Timo Soini and Beppe Grillo have given a public face to populism. The personal cult in populist movements is sometimes so strong that a whole movement and personality become entwined and lose their support if the leading person withdraws from politics. The names and speeches of populist leaders often act as the glue that holds the identity of populist movements together.

Paradoxically, populist leaders seldom come from the "folk" that they claim to represent. Usually, populist leaders are highly educated and quite often also quite wealthy. In other words, they often represent the elite that populist movements protest against. Donald Trump, for example, is a billionaire whose financial assets and social power bear little resemblance to the reference frame of the people he draws the bulk of his support from. Similarly, Marine Le Pen was raised in an upper-class environment and opulent home, acquired a lawyer's education and mainly worked in organisations owned by her father. In her legal career, she initially defended people with little wealth, even illegal immigrants, which makes it hard to believe she is currently the leading figure of France's National Rally.

Populist leaders are generally skilled at presenting. They have a style that connects directly with voters. Many are charismatic speakers and performers, and in this age of social media these populist leaders who are especially skilled and knowledgeable in that arena surge ahead. For example, Donald Trump has been influencing the journalistic news cycle media through his Twitter posts and setting the political agenda. Some populist leaders also use their studies to attract political support, while left-wing populist movements like Kirchnerism in Argentina, Syriza in Greece and Podemos in Spain have exploited Ernesto Laclau's theory of populism during the building of their political parties. The importance of the leader is also emphasised by the previously mentioned fact that populist movements are often strengthened when a long-standing hegemonic bloc of power crumbles and some form of power vacuum occurs. Those populist leaders who then present uncompromising demands receive a great deal of media visibility and, in uncertain times, can build a strong Father or Mother role that creates and offers a sense of security amongst their supporters.

Political identification

Laclau tried to solve the difficulty of defining populism by approaching it as a process rather than as an entity. For Laclau (2005), populism is not an ideology or a specific political movement. In his opinion, it is precisely the attempt to define populism through such fundamental phenomena that leads to problems that make it impossible to arrive at any general definition of populism. According to Laclau, however, populism results from the logic of a political process in which a group of people identify themselves as a political actor. It is a question of once marginal citizens perceiving themselves to be representatives of a forgotten people, which subsequently starts to define themselves as "the people" confronting other groups that are not considered to belong to them. Usually those others represent the so-called old power, political, economic and cultural elites, but also foreigners, immigrants, sexual minorities or supranational corporations. According to Laclau (2005, 94), this is a populist process in which "the plebs, can identify itself with the populus conceived as an ideal totality". Therefore, to Laclau, populism is ultimately about "us and the others", i.e. constructing identities.

The above concept of populism is quite positive as it emphasises the epistemic roots of populism, which refers to popular phenomena widely accepted by the people (Williams 1988, 236–238). The view arises from Laclau's earlier studies with Chantal Mouffe, in which they analyse the emergence of social movements and their power to change politics (Laclau & Mouffe 1985). The view is certainly also influenced by Laclau's own background in Argentina's Peronist Youth movement and left-wing student radicalism in the 1960s. Laclau and Mouffe emphasise the importance of civil society and direct democracy and see party politics as inflexible and part of a rigid system that does not meet people's political demands. They also distinguish between the political and politics (e.g. Laclau & Mouffe 1985; Mouffe 2005a). The former refers to the politicisation of issues that arise from genuine human demands, which can lead to the emergence of controversial issues. The latter refers to the making and management of party politics, which often exists separately from the people's direct political demands.

According to Laclau (2005), in the populist process, there is a well-established hegemonic political system and parties that intersect during a historical situation and context of discontent, which creates the expression of different anti-hegemonic societal and political demands. Although these demands may be ideologically contradictory and seem different from each other, they are linked or "articulated" to each other and generate the opportunity for the creation of a single movement. In this way, for example, traditional left-wing and right-wing distinctions that were previously separable can be unified within the identity creation process of a populist movement, of which the most important factor for the people is the feeling of being heard or "giving power to the people", politicising issues important to oneself and simultaneously creating cohesion for a single political identity. Populism's significance can be considered to have two central aspects for the people: it is affective and mobilising.

Understanding populism as a process of political identification and identity construction is an inventive solution in that it can actually explain all the different forms of populism from right-wing to left-wing populism, from agrarian populism to current populism. However, according to some Laclau critics, the problem with this definition may be that the concept of populism expands to become unanalytical because it covers the politicisation of issues and the formation of political groups on a rather broad scale (Bowman 2007; Arditi 2010). If populism is a confrontation-based political identity that arises by combining societal demands, what creation of political identity is not populism? Some researchers are also clearly disturbed by the possibility of understanding populism in a positive or progressive light (see Hawkins & Kaltwasser 2017, 516). For them, populism always represents the shadowy and ugly side of politics, lies told to the people, unconditional but unattainable promises or extreme rightist nativist ideology, which leads in the worst instances to phenomena such as fascism (cf. Mudde & Kaltwasser 2012a, 15–16).

The rejection of populism simply as a negative phenomenon does not seem to be analytical and justified; however, I believe the criticism of the excessive scope of Laclau's conception of populism is relevant. Despite that, Laclau's populism theory is perhaps the only one that actually covers all the different forms of populism and is able to illuminate the appeal of populism at both the individual and community levels.

Laclau (2005) opens the populist process of identification with the concepts of the empty signifier and the floating signifier, which he takes from anthropologist Claude Lévi-Strauss (1908–2009) and psychoanalyst Jacques Lacan (1901–1981). For example, according to Laclau, "the people" and "the elite" are empty signifiers that have been emptied of solid meanings in a complex reality but which retain the ability to be momentarily filled during the formation of populist opinion, allowing the concept of a unified people to become a political actor. The names of populist leaders and parties and political enemies are also commonly used as signifiers in the construction of populist identity. Empty signifiers are related to floating signifiers, suggesting that the meanings behind expressions are constantly being struggled over and are never entirely settled (Laclau 2005, 133). As Laclau states, in practice, empty and floating signifiers cannot be separated; they are the two sides of the same coin (ibid.).

The starting point for the signifier theory is the semiotics of the Swiss linguist Ferdinand de Saussure (1857–1913), in which he distinguished two levels of linguistic meaning: the signifier and the signified. The signifier is the sign's expression – the spoken or written word – signifying the content that the signifier refers to (Saussure 1960 [1916]). The central insight of de Saussure (1960 [1916]) was that the spoken and written language's signifiers' (words') relationship to the signified content is mainly arbitrary or based on convention. In general, a word has no natural connection to the meaning which it has been associated with throughout its history. This idea was applied to psychoanalysis by Jacques Lacan (1901–1981) with the statement "the unconscious is structured like a language" (Lacan 1977).

According to Lacan, there is no fixed "me" or self. Instead, subjectivity is built on a continuous process of misinterpretations (*méconnaisance*). Thus, we have only a kind of imaginary identification of the self, which is created in interaction in both the real and the imaginary environments (Lacan 1977, 6, 129). As the self is largely based on unconscious mirroring, its foundation is, according to Lacan, a chain of signifiers, which will be built on different interpretations. In other words, we try to construct and maintain a perception of ourselves by continually attaching meanings to the self and thereby making reality and thus ourselves an individual self that is clear and whole. This level of self is called the symbolic order by Lacan and is close to Freud's law of the father. It is in this process that a normal appearing ideology sets us within part of an environment's demands and presents our world relationship as natural (Althusser 1971) – that is how things are and that is how we are (Glynos & Howarth 2007, 118–119). With the aid of the symbolic order, we maintain our sense of self and we are who we think we are, but at the same time we can also become the slaves of the law of the father. As in the Freudian superego, the law of the father can also be harsh and compelling, for example, forcing the self to adapt to the demands of culture and society. On the other hand, identity work can subconsciously create deep pleasure, which is felt in a gratifying manner throughout the entirety of one's body.

Lacanian psychoanalysis explains the pleasure that is created during the populist identification process described by Laclau (2005). Identifying with a group and belonging to imagined people, by means of making a distinction, is an empowering experience in which pleasure can arise by using rational or humorous significations for the confrontations. Pleasure can also be organic, arising, for example, from the subconscious fantasy that the populist group identity allows. Lacan (1977) denotes such pleasure with the term "jouissance", which is an atavistic, corporeal, even orgasmic pleasure that differs from culturally and consciously built "plasir". Perhaps the most obvious jouissance comes from populist humour, in which identifications are strengthened by mocking others. For example, racist humour can support the subconscious fantasies and group identity of nativists in a way that careful reasoning rarely reaches (Billig 2001). However, under the guise of humour, subconscious fantasies can be brought into the light of day via the symbolic order, because humour makes them more acceptable.

Populist opinion formation and group identity are very appealing because they arouse deep emotional experiences. According to

Laclau's theory, the attraction of populism is explained by the fact that it deals with rather fundamental, identity and pleasure-related emotions. Laclau (2005, 101–106) quotes the Slovenian philosopher Slavoj Žižek on the meaning of naming in these experiences. By naming themselves the people, naming enemies (elites, immigrants) and swearing in the name of a leader, they are able to fill empty signifiers while also achieving a fundamentally complete experience as a political actor. According to Žižek (1989, 44), the fantasy of unified wholeness with regard to identity is the principle that defines our concept of reality. The importance of the populist leader is ultimately to be the empty signifier that epitomises the unity of the political identity of the fantasy and around which a group of supporters can form a community. This also explains why the leader is not forced to be charismatic, because the leader's ultimate function is to act as a symbolic point of reference for the community. As early as the 1960s, MacRae (1969, 160) suggested that populism is not ultimately about the economy, politics or even society but about personality in a moral sense. Populism offers the opportunity to be a whole political person during this postmodern era, an era which rips and tears the foundation of the self into fragments and uncertainty.

Psychoanalysis is in itself a very controversial theory and is divided into factions, which also contradict each other. Thus, it is not surprising that Laclau's use of Lacan's psychoanalytic theory has been criticised from different perspectives, even though the explanatory power of psychoanalysis is also believed to open up the unconscious processes behind populism (e.g. Glynos & Stavrakakis 2004; Perelló & Biglieri 2012). Psychoanalysis and Laclau's populist theory explain phenomena that are difficult or even impossible to empirically verify. Notwithstanding the above, the basic tenets of Laclau's thinking are reasonable. Current psychological thinking tends towards a strong consensus that the self is built on continuous interaction with one's environment and that it can be anchored to different values and ideological settings. In everyday terms, populism reaches some kind of human emotional experience that party politics, which is based on rational solutions, is generally not capable of doing. Furthermore, it depends on the respondent's point of view as to whether this is a problem of populism or a broader political problem – or a problem at all.

The psychology of populism is thus based on the possibility it offers to build a stable political identity in today's complex and contradictory world. It creates intense emotional experience in people by appealing to their desire for security, their yearning for a clearly understood world that would not alter and where the elements of identity – nationality, ethnicity, gender, sexuality – would not be the subject of continuous negotiation. However, this does not necessarily mean political stability. On the contrary, some of the appeal of populism comes from the affective experience of the politicising and the challenging of the political *status quo*. Populism offers its supporters their truth. Populism falls if it has to let go of the antagonistic confrontations on which political identity is emotionally built. That is why populism is not a negotiation but a political imperative. It serves a firm belief in the self and in the boundary lines that the subject uses to differentiate oneself from others.

A cultural approach to populism

I began this chapter by introducing Mudde's definition of populism, and continued by introducing various historically emphasised dimensions of populism, which also underpin Mudde's definition. The focus was especially on the ideology, style and movement, the perception of the people and the expression of their will and the alleged confrontation between the forgotten people and other groups of the population, but also in political identifications theorised in Laclaudian tradition (see Table 1.1).

Based on this discussion, three important ideas emerge that are central to the definition of populism. First, it is good to understand populism as a process rather than as an essential phenomenon, such as a political ideology or movement. Because populism invariably involves powerful confrontation, a process better describes the construction of populism. The definition of populism as a form of

Table 1.1 Different definitions of populism

Starting point of the definition	*Key emphasis in definition*	*Actors of definition*	*Recognised theoreticians*
Ideology, heartland	Confrontation between the people and the elite	"The forgotten people"	Cas Mudde, Paul Taggart
Political style	Rhetoric, performance	Politician, political party	Pierre-André Taguieff, Benjamin Moffitt
Political movement	Political grouping, mobilisation	Political party, social movement	Margaret Canovan
Political identification	Political identity, affectivity	Social movement, political group	Ernesto Laclau, Chantal Mouffe

political identification obtained by seeing the world through "us" and "others" covers very different phenomena associated with populism, ideologies, people and movements. Although traditional populism is directed against elites, populists can equally well confront and target other groups of people. Of course, the elite is usually accused of promoting a policy that is too liberal and forgets the privileges of the "people", but more important than the enemy itself is the idea of political identification through affective antagonism.

Second, in relation to the previous point, populism is about politicisation; it is about bringing issues into politics (Palonen 2003). This means that populism cannot be reduced to a question of pure style. The idea of ideology as a reasonably complete system of ideas like capitalism, socialism, liberalism, conservatism or nationalism does not work with populism, yet populism is still ideological: it uses and combines existing ideologies as it requires in order to meet the societal demands of its era and political context. Ideologies are also related to values and moral questions repeatedly expressed within populism. Thus, while populism is very much about expression and performance style, which is based on building an opposition and opposing groups, populism does not exist without some sort of ideological and thus political, underpinnings.

Third, populism is about constructing a political subject, or identities. The influence of populism rests on its ability to deeply influence a group of people and thus create a strong sense of belonging. At the same time, it can also be accompanied by strong negative feelings, even anger, against groups of people who are excluded from the "people" due to the antagonism created. The ideologies in populism are thus related to the justifications used for identifying and constructing identities. As Laclau argues, an important role is played by various signifiers, slogans, names and symbols that can be used to create a sense of belonging and antagonism in this process. On the other hand, the opponents of populism can construct their very own identities from the opposite perspective. Hence, populism is intrinsically linked to the construction of political antagonism in a deep sense of social identity formations.

The ideas above largely echo Ernesto Laclau's and Chantal Mouffe's theorisations. However, the problem with Laclau and Mouffe's populism theory is that it is essentially a theory of all kinds of political awakening, the emergence of political movements and the starting points of political activity, whereas populism has mainly described a certain type of limited political activity. Populism does not have to be understood only negatively or used as a political brawl, but as a concept it loses its ability to be analytical if it refers too broadly to the construction of political self-understanding and identification through the use of antagonisms. According to its etymology, the essence of populism is the perception of common, indivisible people whose will is ignored in politics. Populism is not about pushing the interests of workers or unemployed people, such as in left-wing ideology, or promoting the interests of the middle class or upper class, such as in right-wing ideology. Moreover, it is not about the environmental awareness of a liberal population, such as the green movement, or the defence of conservative Christian, Islamic or Hindu values in the same sense as political movements based on religion. Populism is separated from other politically constructed antagonisms by politicising the idea of "the will of the people" by combining different, even contradictory, interests and ideologies under the same nominator of the people.

As such, populism can be defined as follows:

> Populism is an affective process of political identification, which builds antagonism between two imaginary factions, a misunderstood people and the groups that threaten its sovereignty (elites, immigrants, or other minorities). Populist identification uses ideologically and morally loaded signifiers that are suited to context-laden political demands.

This definition of populism can be called a cultural approach to populism with an emphasis on the rhetorical, performative and discursive dimensions of the populist process combined with a politological perspective on the structures and contexts related to the emergence and practices of populism. It therefore builds a bridge over the gap between ideational and Laclaudian traditions in populism studies that enables a deep theoretical understanding of contemporary populism but also empirical research on the populist called phenomena and movements in party politics, media and democracy. The core of this cultural approach to populism is in the ways populism combines cultural processes of significations – giving politicised meanings to things – and affective identifications – creating social belonging and exclusion – in political identities.

2 A short history of different populisms

If populism is understood according to its most common everyday meaning as the appealing and emotional political rhetoric of the people, populism has existed for as long as there has been politics. Rhetoric was central already to ancient political life and in classical rhetoric, appealing to emotions (*pathos*) was as important as appealing to reason (*logos*) (Aristotle 2004). In the history of modern nation states and political parties, populism has been associated with very varied ideologies and movements. The history of populist movements is usually dated back to the 1870s Tsarist Russia's *Narodniks* and to the 1890s People's Party in the United States (e.g. Canovan 1981; Taggart 2000). However, Wiles (1969, 172) reminds us that the British working-class popular movement Chartism represented typical populism even before the mid-19th century, and even earlier movements associated with the English Civil Wars in the mid-17th century can be considered populist. Thus, what is seen as a populist movement at any given moment is, of course, related to how populism is defined.

Because populist identifications are constructed in a given historical context and local political culture, writing a general history of populism is difficult, if not impossible. The difficulty of defining populism does not make it any simpler. Indeed, the historical modes of populism tend to be extremely context-laden. For example, American, Russian, Latin American and European populism have been discussed as if they were separate phenomena (e.g. Ionescu & Gellner 1969; Taggart 2000). However, in more locally and temporally limited reviews, the history of populism is met to be classified more thematically. Ann-Cathrine Jungar (2017, 20), for example, distinguishes three stages in the history of Nordic populism: the agrarian populism that rose in Finland in the late 1950s, the tax protest populism in Norway and Denmark in the 1970s, and the nativist right-wing populism that has appeared in all the Nordic countries above since the 1980s.

DOI: 10.4324/9781003267539-3

In this book, the history of populism is approached thematically but is still on a general level. I structure the history of populism in relation to the definition of populism presented at the end of the previous chapter, in which populism was understood as the construction of political identities through various confrontational signifying processes. I look at the history of populism first and foremost in relation to the confrontations between forgotten people and their enemies on which populism can be built in any given context. This means that the various forms of populism and populist movements do not rank history entirely chronologically. Some confrontations have been repeated in different contexts throughout history, while others are more clearly fixed to their context. However, viewed in this way, the history of populism can also be structured in periods according to the types of populist confrontations that have been common in specific contexts. This is partly explained by the major social, political and economic cycles that frame the populist identifications and define which ideologies and societal demands are currently linked to each other. Historical changes cause crises in political systems creating space for different types of populism, and populist actors themselves also articulate crises that allow them to present themselves as crisis responses or saviours (Laclau 2005).

Francisco Panizza (2005, 11–13) has identified four factors that he argues contribute to the rise of populism as a central form of political identification. The first is that people no longer believe in the ability of the political system to solve social problems. Secondly, it follows that confidence in political parties and their actions is weak. Third, other changes related to the economy, such as urbanisation or the effects of globalisation, support populist identifications. Fourth, the populist way of structuring the world is spreading to political activity outside political institutions. The increased role of the media in politics contributes to all these factors (Mény & Surel 2002). Thus, politics as well as economic cycles and crises frame the articulations of political ideologies and social demands historically and create space for populism. The history of populism can therefore be understood, at least in part, by looking at the broader structures, currents and changes that frame the various forms of populism. Based on the above, I categorise from the history of modern populism four different forms or steps, namely (1) *agrarian populism*, (2) *authoritarian populism*, (3) *politician's populism* and (4) *new populism* (see Table 2.1).

Agrarian populism is particularly associated with the crises of large agricultural societies in the late 19th century, but its manifestations were also seen in the 1950s and 1960s in countries which rapidly

Table 2.1 Dimensions in historical forms of populism

Form of populism	*Who is the people?*	*The main enemies?*	*Main ideology*
Agrarian populism	Province, heartland	Metropolitan elites	Primitivism, nostalgia
Authoritarian populism	Nation state, the leader	Those who threaten the state rule	Nationalism, law and order
Politician's populism	Forgotten people	Political ruling elite	Antagonism, conservatism
New populism	Native inhabitants, pure people	Ruling elite, globalisation	Manichaeism, nativism

industrialised after the Second World War. Authoritarian populism is associated with the rise of nationalist forces to dominate society as a whole in the first half of the 20th century, especially in Europe, but its manifestations may also be encountered in post-World War South America, Margaret Thatcher's Britain or 21st century Eastern Europe, Trump's United States and Asia (see Norris & Inglehart 2019). Politician's populism rose in the Anglo-American setting in the 19th century, but it has been common, especially since the second half of the 20th century, in Western democracies, and can be encountered in most representative democracies today in which individual politicians seek support from the voters through various media performances. New populism began to strengthen after the 1970s especially in Europe. It is characterised by opposition to elites, but to an increasing extent, the populist movements of the third millennium have opposed immigrants and other minorities. New populism can be linked to the weakening of the decision-making power of nation states caused by globalisation and the growth of the power of transnational corporations, as well as the increased mobility of people. In addition to the West, new populism is also evident in the political cultures of East Asia and South Africa, for example. In politician's populism as well as in agrarian populism, enemies are found within the political system, but in neo-populism they are increasingly found outside it (Figure 2.1).

Agrarian populism

As a form of populism, agrarian populism originates from the structural change of an agrarian society that challenges the living, lifestyles or values of people accustomed to rural communities. Most often agrarian populism derives from the problems of industrialisation and urbanisation for the rural community, but the Narodniki movement,

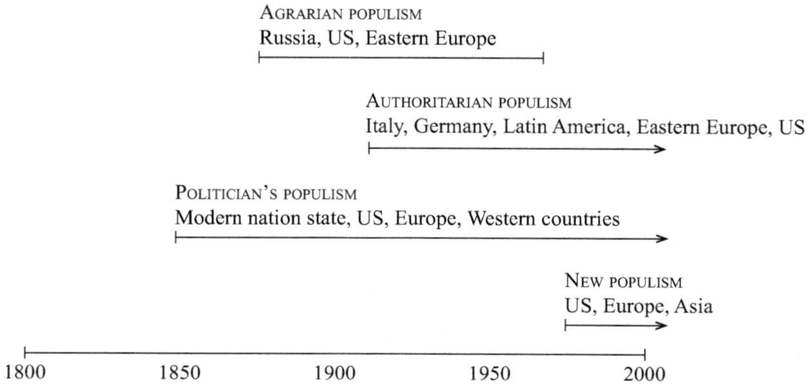

Figure 2.1 The historical forms of modern populism.

one of the earliest forms of modern populism, was more about improving the rights and living conditions of peasants in Tsarist Russia in the 1870s. The name "Narodniki" came from the Russian word for the people and the term "Narodnitšestvo", referring to its ideology, broadly corresponds to populism, even though translation of the term has been a matter of critical discussion (Worsley 1969, 219).

The characteristic of the Narodniks was that the movement was largely formed by leading university intellectuals. The Russian peasants themselves did not form a movement, but the urban intelligentsia adopted the influences of European Marxism at the time and began to apply them to Russian agricultural society (Taggart 2000, 46–47). For example, in 1869, Pyotr Lavrov and Nikolai Mikhailovsky, members of the revolutionary left, published texts that inspired members of the Narodniki movement to spread their message among the peasants. Many views on the Narodniks' interpretations of Marx have appeared as well as their role in Russia's subsequent socialist revolutionary movement, but the movement has invariably been placed in the history of populism (Walicki 1969, 92; Wiles 1969, 172–173).

Although the Narodniks were part of the revolutionary movement, they have been seen as typical representatives of agrarian populism, because they romanticised the rural way of life as part of a Slavophilic ideal and built their ideology on this foundation (Taggart 2000, 46, 57). The American People's Party is a different representative of agrarian populism in this regard. The party was founded in 1892 to advance the interests of the agricultural states of the South and West against the economic policies pursued by the industrialised North and East, but the United States did not really have a peasantry like Russia (Hofstadter 1969, 14–17). Farmers and ranchers were the heirs of slave plantations, capitalist entrepreneurs, who wanted to pursue their own business interests under the pressure of the Democratic and Republican Parties.

The People's Party also differed from the Russian Narodniks in that it was considered a genuine popular movement. The party did not have a clear leadership figure, nor an organised party machinery, but it was formed "from the bottom up" as a protest response to the ruling parties, who were advancing the cause of the new industrial society (Taggart 2000, 26–31). Contrary to the ruling parties, the People's Party demanded farmers' and ranchers' rights for land, railways and funding by building strong confrontations with the plutocracies of the North and East, and thereby it became very popular among South and West farmers (Hofstadter 1969, 18). However, the movement eventually withered away due to deficiencies in organisation and official representation in the party system.

In its rhetoric, the People's Party appealed to the countryside as a mainstay of a true American identity. The idea of a "heartland" is repeated later in American populism as an initial appeal to the people (Taggart 2000, 44). Populism is an integral part of American political culture, regularly raising its head, especially when the nation experiences a sense of crisis. Donald Trump's success in the 2016 presidential election was a clear continuation of the American tradition of agrarian populism. Although Trump relied heavily on disappointment over the unemployment in and politics of industrialised communities, the confrontation he constructed was based on the idea of "true Americanism", which relied to a large extent on nostalgia for a lost heartland. Trump promised to "make America great again", to bring the heartland back. He named the corrupt representatives of the political and monetary authorities of the North and East as his enemies in the same way as the agrarian populist People's Party did 125 years earlier. In this case, however, the populist movement did not emerge from the bottom up but paradoxically was channelled through Trump, who himself represents monetary power.

The agrarian populist movement spread in the wake of the Russian Narodniks to many peasant societies in Eastern Europe. For example, there were similar movements in the Balkans, Bulgaria, Romania, and later in Poland and Hungary, that anticipated other revolutionary movements in the late 19th and early 20th centuries (Ionescu 1969, 99–100). Forms of agrarian populism have been seen even later. For example, the popularity of the Finnish Rural Party (SMP), founded in 1959, as a populist protest movement in the 1960s and 1970s, was largely based on Finland's quite late and rapid industrial revolution after the Second World War. The social restructuring created space for a faction that broke away from the Agrarian Union and opposed the winners of the new social order – the urban elite and the corrupt decision-makers (Helander 1971). SMP promoted the idea of a "real Finnish people", a group who the elite had forgotten in its frenzy for reform and the pursuit of its own interests.

Indeed, theorists of agrarian populism have written that populism is about Jean-Jacques Rousseau's (1712–1778) idea of primitivism that believes in the power of a simple and close-to-nature lifestyle (MacRae 1969, 155). According to MacRae (1969, 160), it promotes a kind of primitive personality whose moral conception is based on the idea of a cohesive and unspoiled rural community. The idea of a primitive personality emphasises the destruction of natural spontaneity on account of the alienating effects of civilisation (MacRae 1969, 161; Wiles 1969, 167). It builds a conservative utopia of the countryside on which an ideal view of man is based. Although such a utopia has been a specific feature of agrarian populism, it can be argued that Trump's 2016 campaign, for example, similarly appealed to a longing for a "real communality" of American small towns and factories. In this way, agrarian populism can become mainstream even in today's democracies.

What is essential in agrarian populism is thus the nostalgic glorification of the countryside and the setting of the lost nation as the signifier of the utopian land of milk and honey. The good old days, the close-knit rural community and working together for a common goal, as well as the alienated urban or cosmopolitan way of life and the selfish pursuit of self-interest, are contrasted. The former is marked by symbols related to agrarian vocabulary and imagery, such as fertile fields and hard-working people, as well as descriptions of a nationalistic nature, the latter marked by vicious urban politicians, selfish employers and machine-like subjugated factory workers. Agrarian populism has been typical in transitions where the countryside is facing strong structural changes, but the nostalgia associated with it may be reflected in other forms of populism too. New right-wing populism emphasising nationalism, in particular, often uses the same types of rhetorical means and markers as agrarian populism when invoking the nation's common past and promoting antagonism between urban cosmopolitan elites and the "pure people" in province. In this case, the heartland of agrarian populism unites with nationalism, in the extreme forms of which the signifier of the people is filled on ethnic grounds and non-native citizens are excluded from the definition.

Authoritarian populism

Many current scholars of populism see it primarily as a political phenomenon related to democracies, but it is clear that populism is also organically linked to fascist and communist extremism, building powerful images of enemies and stirring up outright hatred towards certain groups of people (e.g. Ionescu 1969, 116–118). Under normal circumstances, support for far right movements, for example, tends to remain rather modest, but a deep economic recession increases their popularity because they provide easy enemy images and direct solutions to a difficult situation (see Murdock 2020). For example, the rise of the Nazis from a marginal extremist movement to a ruling political party in 1930s Germany became possible because of a deep depression, when the party was able to provide immediate solutions to the country's weak economic situation and huge unemployment (Hobsbawm 1994). At the same time, Nazis provided security in a situation where many experienced uncertainty and fear about the future.

Indeed, the main characteristic of authoritarian populism is the production of a sense of security in uncertain times (Norris & Inglehart 2019). What is essential here is a strong and persuasive leader who will lead the "forgotten people" out of distress, like Moses did in the Bible. Actually, the religious rhetoric and signifiers are common in his or her performance. Populist leaders are typically attractive performers who act as a kind of father or mother figure for avid supporters. They know how to speak in a direct political language that even ordinary people understand. They provoke and appeal to emotions. Such an appearance is not typical to political negotiation and decision-making, but it does attract public attention and gain support. Every politician can use a populist style at some point in their campaigning, but few build their entire political career on populist appearances. This feature distinguishes the actual populist politician from other politicians.

The fascist extremism that strengthened in Europe in the 1920s and 1930s was built around strong and charismatic leaders. Before they became systems that ruled societies totally and controlled people with coercion and fear, they were heads of small protest movements. However, in the particular historical conjuncture with economic recession, an intense feeling of political powerlessness, the spread of fear and insecurity that affect large crowds, these kinds of policies based on hatred, confrontation and the exclusion of others can spread to a nation-wide mood (Hobsbawm 1994; Murdock 2020). Despair feeds authoritarian populism, as in Italy in the 1920s and Germany in the 1930s.

The personification of populism in the form of a strong charismatic leader has been particularly typical in Latin America. Juan Perón is usually mentioned as a prototype of this kind of leader, rising to leadership in Argentina in the 1940s with the support of his popular wife Maria Eva Duarte (Evita) Perón. Juan Perón took influences from Benito Mussolini in the late 1930s and managed to gain widespread popularity by lifting Argentina from its deep recession by forming alliances with trade unions. The flip side of Perón's revolution was his authoritarian regime, his control of legislation and his restriction of other political actors. Perón's personal influence is reflected in the fact that his socialist reforms and popular movement are called "Peronism" (Taggart 2000, 61–66).

The context of Argentine and Latin American populism in general make them interesting but different from, for example, European populism. The development of democracy has been slow in Latin American countries, where a "clientist" culture based on mutual agreements and power-sharing has overtaken the value of joint decision-making. The United States has also sought to exert a strong influence on the continent because of its economic interests and its fear of the power of socialism. In many countries, there have been major tensions between rural and urban areas, and military dictatorships have taken over when the political system has not been strong and well-established enough. Left-wing populism has often raised its head in response to military regimes and succeeded in building "the people" a political capacity to reform the regime. Indeed, according to Alistair Hennessy (1969, 29), populism is a typical means in Latin America to unite social demands and get people into the movement, regardless of ideology and social class.

Virpi Salojärvi (2016, 185), who studied the connection of populism and media in Venezuela ruled by Hugo Chávez, reminds us that in Latin America, populism often permeates the entire political system when the populist opposition challenges the ruling (populist) power bloc. In other words, a regime that has populistically distanced itself from the former power elite (e.g. a military dictatorship) has since risen to power and gained a hegemonic status, confronted by the new populist opposition. The former, traditional populist movement, receives support among the established working population and the middle class, while the latter new wave of populism emerges from the union of the power-seeking elite and the poorer part of the population (Salojärvi 2016, 82–83). In both forms of populism, the leaders of the movement appear as the key signifiers whose names connect the group's demands to a common political identity (Hennessy 1969, 29). The above narrative supports Ernesto Laclau's (2005) theory of populism and at the same time helps to explain why Argentina-born Laclau ended up structuring populism the way he did.

However, the two-party system includes an innate totalising dimension inherent in populism, as it seeks to cover all political differences and identities through a single confrontation (Palonen 2009, 321). The longing for a strong leader in uncertain times opens up the intermittent success of authoritarian populism in Western democracies as well (Norris & Inglehart 2019). For example, cultural scholar Stuart Hall has analysed Margaret Thatcher's rise to power and popularity in Britain in the 1970s and 1980s by using the concept of authoritarian populism. According to Hall (1988), the popularity of Thatcherism among very different social groups was based on the fact that it combined strict political discipline from above and populist mobilisation from below. Paradoxically, socially disadvantaged groups of people tend to cling to a leader who promises discipline and order, even though discipline often targets them and further oppresses their position. It is explained by the notion of an authoritarian personality, according to which a certain group of people is inclined to adopt conservative and conventional values and believes in destiny, but does not want to question the discipline and is distant or even hostile to humanity itself. The Frankfurt school used an authoritarian personality type to explain the rise of fascism and Nazism in Europe in the 1920s and 1930s (Adorno et al. 1950). They stressed the importance of systematic upbringing and propaganda in the spread of personality type, but it is clear that the general social climate can also affect the popularity of authoritarian populism (Murdock 2020). In this, media and communication technology play a central role.

The ultimate fear raised by populism is generally associated with authoritarian populism. The 20th-century history in Europe has taught that the social atmosphere may turn surprisingly quickly from support for a marginal populist movement to backing for a destructive mass movement that dominates society as a whole. Whether we can no longer talk about populism at a time like this, it depends on how we understand populism. From a human point of view, such a controversy over the definition of populism seems rather pointless, if populism has acted as a pioneer in the development of a repressive totalitarian machinery. In this book, however, I link populism to the scope of democratic political activity and exclude the coercive totalitarianism behind it.

The spectre of authoritarian populism lurks especially in societies where the development of democracy is young or otherwise weak. For example, in the 2010s, authoritarian populism has raised its head in Eastern Europe, where many states were transformed quite rapidly into democracies during the 1990s after the collapse of the socialist system. In these countries, the democratic political systems had not yet had time to properly establish themselves, and it was easier to construct regimes for the actors who dominate the nation with a strict populist grip than in established democracies. In particular, Hungary has faced a development in which the Fidesz party with Prime Minister Viktor Orbán in the chair was adopted a very autocratic command and has started to bridle both the judiciary and the media. Fidesz has gained its support first by confronting its own country's political enemies, but first and foremost by coming to power through a nationalist confrontation with the European Union and non-native Hungarian ethnic groups. On the other hand, it was also a system divided in the same way as in countries that exploited authoritarian populism in Latin America, where two camps were struggling for hegemonic power within the country (Palonen 2009). Similar developments have been seen in other Eastern European countries, notably in Poland, but also to a lesser extent in the Czech Republic and Slovakia, as well as in Turkey, which is quite arbitrarily ruled by Recep Erdoğan (see Gürhanli 2018). Donald Trump's efforts to challenge the US political institutions demonstrated that authoritarian populism may gain foothold also in traditional and strong liberal democracies. Authoritarian populism thus exists in democratic systems, but it can form a bridge to undemocratic forms of government.

Politician's populism

In everyday political language, populism refers above all to a particular political style in which some politicians and parties differentiate themselves from other actors by placing themselves as defenders of the "ordinary people". They present themselves as acting as a kind of inspirer of democracy, at the same time critiquing the frozen representative democracy (see Elmgren 2015). Or, the populist style can be thought of as a mere conscious strategy of political communication that is believed to bring popularity and success in elections. Political scientist Margaret Canovan (2005, 77–78) has spoken specifically of "politician's populism" as a particular personified political style in which the importance of appearances and media publicity has been emphasised. As examples of masters of this style, Canovan uses, among other things, former British Prime Minister Tony Blair and former Italian Prime Minister Silvio Berlusconi.

In politician's populism, the political style is provocative and popular. It appeals in particular to those who see politicians as better-off "professional priests" alienated from the lives of ordinary people and are therefore no longer able to identify with the lives of the disadvantaged. Politicians use difficult foreign words and beat around the bush instead of saying directly what they think. The policies they promote appear to be technocratic and are based on numbers and statistics produced primarily in economic reports and estimates. For those who are not interested in politics, it is difficult to find genuine ideological differences between such politics. The parties appear to be similar, and the voting decisions do not seem to have an impact on the policy pursued. Such politics are followed mainly by the well-educated, but some citizens are indifferent or even feel excluded from the political sphere. Party political participation and turnout are declining (Manin 1997).

In the context of technocratic politics, a populist style based on strong confrontations may seem fresh. Direct claims, sharp expressions and colourful language stand out from the grey mass of political discourse. Painting enemy images gives simple answers and appeals to the emotions of those who have been dissatisfied with politics. What is essential in the politician's populism, however, is that its main enemies are found within the political system. Politician's populism attacks political power holders who have allegedly failed. Thus, its main enemies are other politicians who, according to the populist, have forgotten the ordinary people and who are mainly pushing for their own interests.

By his or her behaviour, the populist becomes a troublemaker within party politics. He promises quick results to complex problems, even though everyone in politics knows that these kinds of answers are unrealistic. On average, politics is slow to make a difference, and the changes achieved are often small and take place over a long period of time. For this reason, designation as a populist is a common political pejorative in many Western democracies (Canovan 2005; Bale et al. 2011). In political discourse, the populist is a deceiver who promises lands and heavens only to gain popularity. However, when populist actors reach a decisive position, they are unable to fulfil their promises and have to eat their words. Because of this negative meaning, the use of the term populism is avoided in public political language use (Herkman 2016). Only a few political actors, who have been successful in political activity, really want to become called populists.

Some populists have tried to make the term more positive in public and emphasised its etymological root in expressions relating to people and popularity (cf. Williams 1988, 236–238). For example, the leader of the Finns Party, Timo Soini, launched the term populism as an integral part of the party's identity before the 2011 parliamentary elections. The party proudly called itself populist in its manifestos, and claimed to speak and advocate for ordinary people (Elmgren 2015, 102–111). By defining populism and talking about "old parties", the Finns Party also strategically distinguished themselves from other parties that had been in power for a long time and were thus able to build a self-image as an alternative protest movement. When the party won the election and consolidated its position in parliament and later also in government, the talk of populism was largely forgotten. Despite Soini's attempts, the main meaning of populism did not change in public discourse, and the established movement no longer wanted to identify itself as populist (cf. Herkman 2016).

In a sense, politician's populism can be linked to all populism because political populism is usually channelled through some politicians. A populist-style politician becomes a symbol of a political movement whose name serves as a central signifier uniting identifications to the movement. This explains why populism is so often associated solely with a charismatic leadership, even though populism by definition is more broadly a process of politicisation and group formation. However, it is also possible to treat the politician's populism as a historically specific form of populism in the sense that not all politicians' populist outcomes lead to the formation of new political groups, let alone political movements. Politician's populism may be rather just a provocative political style within the party system, and it can also be practised by politicians who have established themselves and represent traditional parties.

Historically, the politician's populism has been associated especially with particular political cultures, where snappy rhetoric and style are an integral part of politics. Politician's populism has been, for example, an integral part of the two-party systems of Britain and the United States. Strong political confrontation and dissociation seem to belong to such a system, which makes the populist style a "natural part" of politics (cf. Palonen 2009). In both countries, the politician's populism raises its head from time to time – the most recent examples being the political struggle that preceded the Brexit vote and Donald Trump's vote for presidency during 2016. Politician's populism has also played an important role in more authoritarian regimes in which two populist movements have struggled for hegemonic power, as in some Eastern European and Latin American countries (e.g. Palonen 2009; Salojärvi 2016), as well as in countries such as France and Italy, where societies in general are more polarised and politically more controversial than, for example, in consensus-seeking Central and Northern Europe (see Hallin & Mancini 2004).

However, the politician's populism has regularly raised its head in established multi-party democracies since the late 20th century. Taggart and Szczerbiak (2002, 34–35) have argued that the popularity of populist anti-EU parties, for example, in European multi-party democracies is understandable because it is easy for small protest parties to construct their own identity and stand out from the demarcated themes of the traditional parties in such an environment. The multi-party democracies in Central and Northern Europe have also been quite consensual, at least since the Second World War. In them, decision-making has been based on the pursuit of a broad consensus, allowing populist movements to easily bundle ruling parties into one corrupt cartel against which they can build their own identity.

Thus, the politician's populism has been and continues to be an integral part of modern representative democracy, where the populist style periodically serves as a tool not only for political differentiation but also for the politicisation of issues. Most successful politicians harness a populist style at some point in their careers as a tool for political campaigning. The early stages of contemporary established political parties have also been quite populist in their style because the identity of the movement has been constructed through striking confrontations. The political environment of the 21st century seems to favour politician's populism very strongly, as there are an increasing number of voters in many countries who feel that ruling politicians and parties do not meet their social demands, and in changing the media environment and mediatised politics the politician's populism in particular gains a favourable resonance.

New populism

In the second half of the 20th century, populism, especially in the West, has often come to be called new populism or neo-populism to mark a difference between the earlier agrarian and totalitarian forms of populism. Taggart (2000, 73, 86) sees opposing political institutions and even anti-politics to be a unifying feature of various new populist movements. A great part of contemporary study equates new populism primarily with radical right-wing populism, which emphasises extremism, nativism and xenophobia as its engines of political identification and mobilisation (e.g. Mazzoleni et al. 2003; Mudde 2007; Rydgren 2010).

It is true that all new populist political parties have their origins in protest movements that strongly attack old parties and the ruling elite, but it is an exaggeration to claim that they would be opposed to politics or the political system itself. Many new populist movements often differ from extremist movements precisely in that they function as part of party democracy and are also closely linked to it. Especially in Europe, new populist parties have established their position in the party field by this millennium at the latest and been active in national representative institutions and even governments (e.g. Albertazzi & McDonnell 2008; Akkerman et al. 2016). In fact, all the European populist movements listed at the beginning of the book are these kinds of new populist parties. On the other hand, many of these parties have links to extremist movements, and the parties influence people who belong or have belonged to extremism. Extremist movements can also increase their support through populist logic, and populist parties channel the support of extremist movements through representative democracy. Thus, sometimes the difference between the populist side and an extremist movement can be blurred.

Not all new populist parties are right-wing radical nationalists. The neo-populist spirit of protest and opposition to incumbent power may be as attached to left-wing ideology and directed against corporations and elites of monetary power, as in the case of the Spanish Podemos party or the Greek Syriza. The protest may also target old political parties in general, claiming that they are unable to provide solutions to the key social problems of the third millennium. New populism has emerged in most Western countries in response to the crisis of party politics, with a sufficient number of people feeling that they have been left out of politics. At the same time, new populists are themselves adept at inciting a spirit of protest and crisis thinking, which increases their support. The solutions they offer to the crisis, in turn, depend on the local context.

Alongside their consolidation, the protest spirit of new populist movements often eases, the most radical members of movements are dismissed, and parties begin to conform to traditional party political culture. As movements develop their party organisations and operate in the institutions of representative democracy, the system seems to assimilate them into itself. The transformation into decent political parties suggests that populism emphasising confrontations is a common phenomenon particularly in the process of the emergence of political movements. On the other hand, many new European populist parties have also been able to maintain their populist character as a countermovement, even though they have gained a fairly well-established position among other parties (Akkerman et al. 2016). Indeed, Andrej Zaslove (2008) argues that populist parties have become established players in European party politics in this millennium. Populism as such has seemed to be mainstream in the 21st century.

The success of neo-populist movements in Western democracies is explained more by the political context of the time than by a general anti-democratic spirit or extremist nationalism. The latter are contextual symptoms rather than causes. All new populist parties are fed by a soil where globalisation has challenged the political capacity of nation states. This also applies to the rise of populism in Asia and Africa in this millennium (Hadiz & Chryssogelos 2017). Industries are constantly looking for cheaper production and labour costs regardless of state borders, which radically changes the economic structures and labour markets of nation states. At the same time, technological developments including digitalisation, networking, automation and robotisation are changing the structures of workforces and businesses and making countries compete with each other on education, know-how and competitiveness. Together with changes in media and communication environments these transformations have constituted fertile soil for the spread of populism.

Various crises in the Middle East, Africa, the Caucasus and Asia have created refugee flows, and people are moving more vigorously from one country to another in the hope of a safer and better life. Knowledge of other countries and their living conditions as well as various ideologies, beliefs, opinions and extremism that act as stimuli for political movement, activism and even terrorism are spreading in the blink of an eye through social media and the Internet. Today, different people, ideas and cultures collide on a completely different scale than in the 1970s, for example, which adds to the uncertainty of many about the stability of identities and life in general. The world seems to be in a very mobile state compared to the world order a few decades ago, first defined by the Cold War confrontation between the US-led Western world and the Soviet-led Eastern Bloc. This was subsequently characterised by the philosopher Francis Fukuyama (1992) as the "end of history", meaning that since the early 1990s market capitalism had become integrated into liberal democracy around the world. However, history did not end, but the current world order, riding from "crisis-to-crisis", seems to feed particularly well populist confrontations that offer simple answers to complex problems and would appear to provide order in chaos.

In many Western democracies, the rise of new populism is also associated with the challenges faced by the welfare state (see Taggart

2000, 75). For example, in the Nordic countries, the earliest wave of new populism was connected to strong industrialisation and urbanisation in Finland in the 1960s and 1970s, and to building a welfare state with strong taxation in the 1970s, especially in Denmark and Norway. Populist parties opposed taxation and state interventions. However, the parties did not become very popular, and such libertarian populism withered away quite quickly as the welfare state proved to be a fairly successful project. Rather, current Nordic populism is a reaction to the dismantling of welfare state structures in the 21st century (Herkman 2017a). People are accustomed to a secure life, and increased global competition is making it increasingly difficult to maintain a welfare state. At the same time, wholesale decision-making power has shifted from national political institutions to multinational business corporations and transnational alliances, such as the European Union. The room for manoeuvre in national politics has shrunk significantly, crunching party-political systems and creating room for populist movements that challenge policymakers with legitimation problems and promise to return decision-making back to the national level.

Neo-populist movements flourished in the Nordic countries at the turn of the millennium, when they embraced right-wing radical anti-immigration and nationalism as their central themes. For those who experience insecurity and are tired of politics, these movements provide a clear explanation and a simple solution to the welfare problems of the nation state. The political environment at the beginning of the third millennium supports such an appeal. Increased immigration is easy to link to industrial and economic structural changes, the cause of which is to be found in the aforementioned economic globalisation currents and technological developments. In some other countries, such as Spain and Greece, populist articulations are emphasised differently because of their contexts. Left-wing economic policy confrontation seems to meet the needs of populist identifications better than ethnicity-based antagonisms in countries that have not built a strong welfare state safety net and where "clientist" or corrupt governance cultures collide with transnational markets and austerity demands promoted by European Union. As of this writing, there is no sign that populist articulations will disappear. After a brief golden era of welfare states, the world seems to face a situation where there is plenty of room for new populist identifications also in the Western democracies.

3 Populism and democracy

The relationship between populism and democracy is complex, and it has been explored from various angles with no clear results. Some scholars link populism to authoritarian and totalitarian regimes such as Fascism, Nazism and Communism; others think that populism is essentially democratic in its nature. Even if I recognise the tendencies in populism that lead to authoritarianism, populism is here explored largely as a democratic phenomenon. As discussed in the previous chapter, populism can be – and has historically been – connected to authoritarian regimes, but populism is first and foremost part of democracy in the sense that its very foundation lies in the idea of the "sovereignty of the people" (see Canovan 2005). Authoritarian rulers and totalitarian regimes may apply a populist style, but populism as a genuine political identification and form of politicisation can be realised only if there are possibilities for these kinds of processes. In a totally authoritarian system or under dictatorships there is no room for these kinds of counter-hegemonic political identifications.

The inherent connection between populism and democracy is also seen in the etymology of these very terms. Whereas populism derives from the Latin word "populus", democracy comes from the Greek word "demos", both meaning the people. Democracy literally means "the power of the people" ("kratos" means power). Thus, in its simplest form, democracy refers to the sovereignty of the people and the majority rule in politics – very similar to populist identifications (Mudde & Kaltwasser 2012a, 10). In other words, democracy differs from monarchy, empire, dictatorship, totalitarianism or any other regime in which an individual or small and uncontested power clique rules over those who are obedient to them. Nevertheless, as was discussed in Chapter 1, who are included in the people and how "the will of the people" is implemented, varies historically and between democracies. Therefore,

DOI: 10.4324/9781003267539-4

the forms and consequences of populism are also linked to contextual differences between democracies.

When democracy is discussed in the 21st century, usually representative democracy and liberal democracy are self-evident starting points. These are the forms of democracy where contemporary populism flourishes, even though populism can also appear in other kinds of societal settings. In addition, populism as a concept has been linked to the ideas of "radical democracy" or "counter-democracy", especially opposing ideals of consensual democracy and deliberative democracy. Populist identifications should always be considered in the context in which they appear. Therefore, I will next briefly open up these various concepts of democracy in which contemporary populism is in different ways intertwined.

Different forms of democracy

After the Second World War Austrian-born economist and social scientist Joseph Schumpeter (1883–1950) defined democracy as institutional organisation of political decision-making that makes the people a source of these decisions by elections in which individual representatives are elected to promote the people's will (Schumpeter 1949, 250). The definition is widely used, but it is fairly practical and displays especially representative democracies in which decision-making is based on the mandate achieved by voting in elections (Mudde & Kaltwasser 2012a, 11). In this sense Schumpeterian democracy is in fact a definition of Western society rather than democracy as such. However, these societies create fertile soil for populism.

Many scholars link populism above all to representative democracies (see Canovan 1999; Mény & Surel 2002; Taggart 2002). According to them, populism provides a particular response to the problems of representative democracy. If representatives do not have enough support among citizens or citizens do not think that they represent "the will of the people" fully enough, the legitimacy of representation crumbles and populist identifications become tempting (Mény & Surel 2002, 13–14). Taggart (2002) calls populism a disease or a symptom of problems in representative democracy. Typically, populism attacks alleged corruption in representative democracy and demands direct democracy that gives the power directly to the people. Paradoxically, many populist movements rely on strong leadership, even though they long for direct power for the people (Mény & Surel 2002, 8–11). However, as Francisco Panizza (2005, 18–19) reminds us, the role of a populist leader is mostly to serve as a uniting signifier for populist identifications. For supporters, a populist leader represents everything that the "corrupt elite" of representative democracy does not.

The idea of direct democracy stresses that citizens should involve themselves in societal decision-making. Populists typically demand the increasing use of referendums, however after gaining power they often make rather leader-centric or central-planned decisions by justifying that, unlike other representatives, their leading figures really represent the people. This demonstrates that the relationship between populism and representative democracy is contradictory. On the one hand, populism derives from the general critique of the representative democracy and from the demand of direct representation of "the pure people". On the other hand, it constructs powerful confrontations between various groups, excludes some groupings from the people and promotes easily authoritarian rule.

Some political theories connect populism to the idea of radical democracy because populism challenges the *status quo* of representative democracy. Radical democracy means a normative ideal in which continuous political contestations and changes in representation are valued and conventional representative democracy seems politically withered and stagnated (see Fenton 2016). It is true that representative democracies tend to find their ways towards hegemonic *status quo*, in which power and decision-making start to look self-evident and routine-like. In this kind of development citizens become passive, losing their enthusiasm for politics in which real choices do not seem to be offered. Stagnatisation is common both in liberal democracies and in more authoritarian systems. The ideal of radical democracy opposes all forms of political stagnatisation. It stresses that democracy is healthier if people have genuine political interests and these interests are enthusiastically pursued, meaning that they become politicised.

Ernesto Laclau and Chantal Mouffe (1985) have been central proponents of the radical democracy theory. Especially Mouffe (2002) has promoted so-called agonist democracy, in which conflicting ideologies and views live together, even if they do not meet each other. Agonism differs from antagonism that leads to possibly violent confrontations. The Mouffean idea of agonism criticises especially the normative ideal of "deliberative democracy", represented most famously by German philosopher Jürgen Habermas, whose theories of political public sphere and communicative action emphasise the constructive dialogue between conflicting social interests. In the Habermasian (1989) ideal form of the public sphere, different interests are represented in public deliberation, in which the best argument ultimately wins and a common opinion is formed to guide the social decision-making. In an optimised situation, societal consensus is achieved through public deliberation.

Critics have reminded us that politics is not just rational argumentation or deliberation. According to them, the ideal of deliberation does not take into account affectivity and irrationality in politics, which often derive from unconscious needs and political identities rather than from cool rationality (e.g. Fraser 1992). This is why Mouffe (2005a, 88–89) separates "the political" from "politics". The former means political confrontations and the politicisation of issues deriving from people's own interests, whereas the latter signifies the working of the political system and its institutions that represent *status quo* in society. According to Mouffe, consensus destroys the political and emphasises the politics as conventional and institutional agreements between political parties. Thus, the role of populism is to bring political and politicisation back to social engagement.

Laclau's (2005) theory on populism is based on his explanation on the formation and mobilisation of social movements developed together with Mouffe in the 1980s. According to Laclau and Mouffe (1985), genuine social movements are formed in a context in which hegemonic politics does not sufficiently meet the needs and problems of the people. A counter-hegemonic movement is born to combine various context-laden social demands under the same umbrella. These demands may even be ideologically contradictory and do not necessary follow the class structure in society. However, it is important that different demands can be linked or "articulated" to each other, and through this articulation a unity of counter-hegemonic group identification is constructed. This is why Lauclau's and Mouffe's theory is also called "articulation theory".

In the Laclaudian tradition populist logic is reminiscent of general logic of all social movements, because politicisation is a constitutive force in populist identification. Therefore, according to Laclau and Mouffe, populism is also essential in radical democracy theory because it challenges the societal *status quo*. However, as Laclau's critics have reminded us, all that is political or involved in politicisation is not populism (Bowman 2007; Arditi 2010; Moffitt 2020). I agree with the critics that it is good to reserve populism for a particular type of politicisation, namely identifications with "the people" as opposed to groups that allegedly threaten their sovereignty. Otherwise populism loses its analytical power as a concept and begins to signify almost anything in politics (Arditi 2010).

Another dimension in Laclau and Mouffe's theory that has been criticised is their positive stance towards populism. This is originally connected to their radical democratic theory about the progressive possibilities of radical leftist social movements. The critics do not want to adopt this normative utopia based on radical democratic populism theory (Hawkins & Kaltwasser 2017; Moffitt 2020). Instead, many scholars see especially contemporary right-wing populism as rather negative and as even a harmful phenomenon for democracy (see Panizza 2005). However, one has to keep in mind that even among radical democratic theory, not all scholars promote the progressive potential of populism. The French political scientist Pierre Rosanvallon (2008), for example, has talked about "counter democracy", meaning a necessary suspicion of representative democracy, manifesting itself in activism, demonstrations and life politics. However, even if Rosanvallon (2008) connects populism to the very same suspicion against the class structure-based party politics that cannot respond to people's social demands in contemporary representative democracies, he does not see it as such a progressive counter-democratic force as civil commotion. Quite the contrary, Rosanvallon defines populism rather negatively as an activity that is based on hatred and false judgements that even promotes violent confrontation.

Politician's populism and new populism are therefore common in representative democracy that have both liberal and authoritarian forms (see Figure 3.1). For example, Vladimir Putin's Russia is a representative democracy with regular national and presidential elections, and it can also be formally linked to liberal democracies with the constitution securing citizens' rights. However, Russia is an authoritarian nation where real possibilities for political opposition, free press and

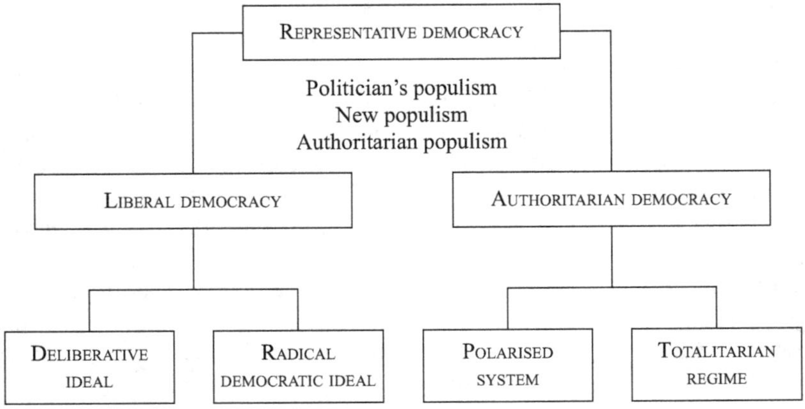

Figure 3.1 Forms of democracy and populism.

challenging Putin's regime are practically non-existent, and minority rights are also trampled on. This kind of centralised power is typical to authoritarian democracies in which rulers exploit populist nationalism to strengthen and maintain their power. In addition to Putin, Erdoğan in Turkey and Orbán in Hungary have applied authoritarian populist strategies in Europe today.

In some liberal democracies, such as the United States and France, presidential power is also remarkable, but in these countries checks and balances – institutions like political structures, laws and courts as well as the press and political opposition – control authoritarian tendencies (Mudde & Kaltwasser 2012a). Moreover, in elections real changes are possible, as was seen in the United States where Donald Trump could not re-elected in the 2020 elections. In addition, liberal democracies can be divided into representatives of deliberative and radical democratic ideals. The former emphasises societal consensus and transparency in decision-making, the latter individualist representation, political contestation and pluralism (see Hallin & Mancini 2004). Deliberative ideals have been strong especially in North and Central European countries after the Second World War, and a more radical democratic approach has been favoured in Southern European and Anglo-American countries. In deliberative democracies, populists have usually been regarded as political troublemakers, disturbing consensual decision-making. However, from a radical democratic perspective populism has appeared to be more normal and has even been politically reformist (see Moffitt 2020). This has also been seen in scholars' normative approaches to populism. American scholars seem to have been – at least before Trump – a more positive attitude towards populism than Europeans, who in past history have seen democratic populism turn into authoritarian and even totalitarian regimes in their own and neighbouring countries.

Political power is centralised and opposition cornered in authoritarian democracies, but in some cases populism might serve as a counter-hegemonic challenger to the ruling power. This has been seen historically especially in Latin America, where populist movements have been organised from the bottom-up to challenge hegemonic power (Taggart 2000; Levitsky & Loxton 2012). Often these movements have been led by a charismatic figure who provides symbolic cement in uniting populist identifications and mobilisations. However, when counter-hegemonic movements achieve power, sometimes after painful revolutionary battles, they typically turn into hegemonic authoritarian regimes. A new counter-hegemonic populist movement arises and begins to challenge the older one, which loses its power as a signifier of affective populist identification. This kind of dialectic is common in polarised political systems (Palonen 2009). However, in the worst scenarios, authoritarian populism and democracy turn into totalitarian systems that ban opposing ideologies or repress dissidence by coercive means. In these cases we can no longer talk about democracy or populism, because contesting political identifications become totally impossible.

Populism as a challenge to liberal democracy

Populism can be seen first and foremost as a process that originates in the distrust of representative democracy. Populism articulates the social demands of those who think of forming a group of "forgotten people". Representative democracy has often been associated with liberal democracy, which became the leading model of society, especially in the Western world, after the Second World War, because it was thought to serve as the best inoculation against horrible disasters such as the two world wars at the beginning of the 20th century. In liberal democracy, free elections and parliamentarianism are supplemented especially by various civil and citizen rights, such as general human rights and the aspiration to equality, minority rights, freedom of speech and the right to express various ideological, political and religious attitudes (Mudde & Kaltwasser 2012a, 11–13). Sometimes liberal democracies are also called constitutional democracies on account of the civil rights generally being written into the constitution (Mény & Surel 2002, 8–11).

Populism has been linked intrinsically to liberal democracies for two reasons. Firstly, liberal democracies create a political environment in which, paradoxically, populist identification become possible. In fact, the political climate in liberal democracies supports the idea of criticism and challenges the centralisation of political power. In authoritarian systems this kind of critique of political power is often tyrannously oppressed. Secondly, in addition to the minimal requirements of representative democracy – free elections and elected representatives – liberal democracy defends minority rights by means of a constitution. Populism, in turn, appeals to "majority rule" and is therefore often a confrontational force in liberal democracies (Mudde & Kaltwasser 2012a, 17).

It is of little surprise that particularly in Western liberal democracies populism has generally applied nationalist and nativist ideologies combined with conservative values in its identifications. Consequently it has often appeared in the form of radical right-wing populism, because it constructs a clear counter-hegemonic force in the liberal democratic environment. In more conservative environments these kinds of values are not so apparent in populist identifications. In developing or poorer countries populist identification is often articulated more strictly with economic demands to improve the living conditions of the people (Mudde & Kaltwasser 2012b, 207). European liberal democracies have been traditionally successful welfare states in which nativist right-wing populism has flourished, but in Latin America, for example, populism has been linked more often to leftist demands for economic equality with no clear ethnic dimensions (see Taggart 2000, 60; Levitsky & Loxton 2012, 161).

According to the ideal of deliberative democracy, various groupings in society negotiate their interests and deliberate together to gain the best political decisions with large societal support. Many North and Central European liberal democracies have strived for this ideal after the Second World War and can therefore also be called "consensus democracies" (Mudde & Kaltwasser 2012a, 15). In the Nordic and Benelux countries, for example, the principle of equality and welfare state ideology have served as a strong backbone for consensual decision-making. It seems rather surprising that particularly in these countries populist political parties have a long history and nativist right-wing populist movements have been especially successful in the 21st century. However, the above-mentioned tendency in populist articulations explains the development: in liberal consensus democracies right-wing populist identifications are easy to equate with nativist-conservative articulations and antagonism against consensual elites that are labelled as a corrupt and far too liberal cartel that undermines "the pure people".

Populism is based on confrontation and is therefore inherently anti-deliberative. In populism the alleged majority view is used for self-legitimation at the cost of pluralism. In the populist approach, deliberation on minority rights is seen as nonsense. It is particularly this contradiction between majority rule and minority rights that puts populism and liberal democracy on a collision course and sometimes makes populists resist the constitution (Mudde & Kaltwasser 2012a, 17). The constitution treats all individuals or citizens as equals, but according to nativist right-wing populists, ethnic minorities do not deserve the same rights as native inhabitants. Many successful right-wing populist actors have therefore promoted "welfare chauvinism" in which social security benefits should be distributed differently between native inhabitants and immigrants (see Bay et al. 2013).

Right-wing populist actors see the constitution as their enemy, because it protects minority rights and prevents them from adopting the reforms they have promised to their voters, or at least it complicates these processes. Therefore, it is not surprising that many populist actors try to change the constitution in a way that allows them a more direct exercise of power. This has happened in Hungary and Poland, for example, but the critique against the constitution has also increased in many Western liberal democracies in which right-wing populist parties have been successful during the 21st century. In general, the constitution may appear rigid and may block legislation work among politicians but that, indeed, is its purpose. The constitution is a lesson learned from the world wars. It slows down decision-making to guarantee equal rights for everybody and to stop a single actor achieving too much power. The constitution is an inherent element of democracy, keeping decision-making and legislation processes as transparent and pluralistic as possible.

In addition to the constitution, liberal democracies contain other institutions (checks and balances) that control politics, such as courts of law and the free press. Therefore, populist actors often also attack those institutions that they label as part of the corrupt elite. The Law and Justice Party in Poland and Donald Trump in the United States have constantly blamed the media and the court of law and tried to change these to proponents of their regimes. In fact, these kinds of attacks test the strength of liberal democracy. As long as checks and balances repel illiberal offensives, liberal democracies can survive. If they give in to populist demands to change the political, juridical and media systems, the path towards authoritarianism is open. This has been seen, for example, in Recep Erdoğan's Turkey and in Viktor Orbán's Hungary, where populist demands of direct democracy have turned to rather authoritarian regimes during the 2010s. In authoritarianism minorities and opposition lose their rights and voices. In this situation one may ask if it is even possible to talk any more about populism, or is it rather a question of autocracy and propaganda.

Populism as part of democracy

Obviously, populism is organically linked to democracy, but the challenges it poses to liberal democracy have made it a negative term and phenomenon according to many thinkers (Norris & Inglehart 2019). Populism is a problem for liberal democracy because it is nonliberal (Canovan 1999, 7) or illiberal (Pappas 2019). Populism has therefore been called a syndrome, a disease or a symptom of democracy (see Wiles 1969; Taggart 2002; Arditi 2005; Rosanvallon 2008). More neutrally, Margaret Canovan (1999) calls populism a shadow of democracy. In a way, populism is another side of the coin, an inevitable dimension of democracy, because both populism and democracy gather their strength from the sovereignty of the people and, as discussed in Chapter 1, the people is a very vague concept. The people and its sovereignty are always constructions made from a particular point of view (Panizza 2005, 29).

Like democracy, populism calls for a civil society and the will of the people to support the political system. Populism to some extent repeats the same ideals as democracy. Canovan (1999, 8–14) argues that populism follows democracy like a shadow because of two ambivalent dimensions in democracy: a "redemptive vision" of a better and more pragmatic organisation of governance. Thus, on the one hand democracy promises redemption, on the other hand it serves everyday political routines. The latter means political institutions, administration and regulation; the former encourages citizens to challenge these institutions through spontaneous and direct political activity. This Janus-faced democracy between civil society and party politics motivates populism and counter-democracy (Rosanvallon 2008).

Populism seems problematic because it does not follow the institutional traditions, rules and rituals of democracy even if it harnesses the central democratic values of civil engagement and the people's will. Benjamin Arditi (2005, 90–91) describes populism as a democracy's drunken dinner guest who makes trouble but cannot be asked to leave the table. The main problem originates in the fact that populism cannot serve a functional option to representative democracy without turning into an authoritarian regime (Mény & Surel 2002, 18). Populism presents itself as the voice of the whole people in the name of the majority (Canovan 2005, 88). However, no group can ever represent the whole people, meaning that the coexistence of various interest groups is the lifeblood of any democracy. The people in populism are always just a part of it, often representing the minority in the population, but promoting itself as the whole people.

Thus, the populism/democracy relationship is mutual. On the one hand, populism affects democracy, and on the other hand, democracy frames populism and its implementations. Politicians' populism may either refresh stagnated party politics or it can direct politics to sidetracks. Nevertheless, the impact of politicians' populism is seldom revolutionary. However, if populism really challenges the party field it may have a deeper influence on party politics and democracy. This has been seen in many European countries in which populist parties have radically changed the power-relations of traditional political parties, and the decision-making in re-organised government/

opposition conjunctions has become complicated. The most revolutionary influence on democracy is if the populist actor gains a majority ruling status in society and starts to emphasise its authoritarian regime by challenging liberal democratic checks and balances, as has happened in Hungary and in Poland during the 2010s and also in Donald Trump's United States. These developments demonstrate that populism is an inherent part of democracy and may either work as a corrective or as an ultimate threat to it, shaking the very existence of liberal democracy.

Threats and correctives

Populism is seen more often as a threat than as a possibility for democracy, because populism in most cultures and languages is a negative term, whereas democracy on the other hand has positive meanings (Mudde & Kaltwasser 2012a, 15). In political discourse populism is pejorative, signifying an excessive and provocative style, empty promises and demagogic wooing of voters (e.g. Bale et al. 2011). In public debates populism is often linked to nativist right-wing populism with extreme nationalist and xenophobic or even racist rhetoric, confronting human rights, equality and minority rights generally promoted in liberal democracies and the journalistic media. Thus, in public and political discussions populism is seldom valued.

However, some scholars have reminded us that populism may work as a corrective to democracy if the ruling elite has become estranged from the everyday life of their voters and cannot sufficiently address their problems and experiences (Mény & Surel 2002, 14–15). Populism can possibly give a voice to those who find themselves to be excluded from politics and feel that nobody represents their interests. As such, populism may mobilise citizens who have got bored with stagnated politics and have alerted politicians to focus on their needs more intensively. It is possible that populism even activates citizens and voters who have not been interested in politics before (Mudde & Kaltwasser 2012a, 21). Panizza (2005, 11) reminds us that, thanks to populism, some people might find their political identities and experience political subjectivity for the first time in their life. The success of populist political parties in elections around the world indicates that there has been a large demand for political populism in the contemporary political and social conjuncture.

A simple explanation for the large-scale appeal of populism may come from the populist communication style that invokes emotions and passion and applies clear and popular vocabulary. Compared to professional politicians' technocratic and bureaucratic language that echoes the daily agenda and terminology of economy, justice and other social institutions, populist rhetoric is very different and seems fresh (Mudde & Kaltwasser 2012a, 21). Populism can make a difference and bring politicisation back to politics that has previously been experienced as apolitical management. As a politicisating mode, populist rhetoric enforces political identifications and mobilisations in times of increasing voter apathy.

In addition to rhetoric, populism is always linked to real societal demands deriving from particular contexts. Often traditional political actors do not – for one reason or another – discuss these issues eagerly, or they cannot address the issues with proper language. As populism does not follow traditional left/right class structures but combines or articulates different social demands and ideologies to each other from a popular basis (Laclau 1977), it is a more fluid and quicker tool in responding to context-laden social problems than ideology-bound traditional party politics. As such, populist movements can put pressure on other parties to crystallising their ideological underpinnings and to better differentiate themselves in the party field.

The threat caused by populism derives from its tendency to banalise the social order of representative democracy, and in extreme cases this can threaten the very existence of democracy. According to Taggart (2002, 76), populism simplifies political debates in a dangerous way, because a seemingly fresh and direct populist appeal to the people very easily turns into simple antagonism and the exclusion of outgroups essential for populist affective identification. Populism changes the complex political reality to a straightforward black and white constellation with no shades of grey. This is both the powerful attraction and the drawback of populism that is realised when populist actors gain success in elections: pluralist democratic decision-making inevitably involves negotiation and compromises that do not support a populist Manichean black and white approach. This is why populist actors cannot usually keep their promises after electoral success and make their supporters even more disappointed in politics.

Populist movements are therefore under pressure to push towards illiberal politics that leads to the crumbling of democratic institutions. In the name of the alleged majority they promote policy oppressing minorities and therefore challenge the diversity and pluralism essential to liberal democracy. Thus, populism might inflame the whole political discussion and make social decision-making challenging or even impossible (Mudde & Kaltwasser 2012a, 21). This kind of development has been seen in such European liberal democracies as in

Sweden, Switzerland, Austria and Belgium, in which success of radical right-wing populist parties has complicated government coalitions' work during the 2010s, and in the United States where Donald Trump's presidency made collaboration between the Congress and the Senate even more fraught than before. Even if one does not adopt the consensual ideal of deliberative democracy one must admit that the organisation of societal life is difficult if political decision-making proves impossible because of unassailable confrontations.

The greatest fear of populism pertains to historical developments in which populist appeals have turned regimes authoritarian. If hostile populist actors promote direct democracy and majority rule against the liberal democracy and this is complemented with their absolute majority in political institutions, they may begin to modify authoritarian systems. The viability of democracy is tested in its ability to resist these efforts and is linked to the checks and balances of societal institutions and to citizens' willingness to maintain the democratic order. The history of Fascism, Nazism and Communism provides a necessary reminder of authoritarian populism and its link with totalitarian regimes capable of atrocities.

Mudde and Kaltwasser (2012b) conclude their work by considering various case analyses on the role of populism, which can often be both a threat and a support to democracy. Because democracies are different, the forms of populism also vary depending on the contexts making the consequences context-laden. The mutual relationship between populism and democracy affects the forms and effects of the populism/democracy connection. According to Mudde and Kaltwasser's (2012b, 210–211) concluding remarks, in established welfare states such as Austria, Belgium and Canada, liberal democratic institutions have been so strong that right-wing populism has hardly shaken their foundations. Instead, in Eastern European and Latin American countries included in the analyses the democratic institutions and traditions are much weaker and therefore the system level effects of populism have been stronger than in traditional liberal democracies.

In many Central Eastern European countries with a communist past the populist-oriented regimes have turned authoritarian during the 21st century, because liberal democratic regimes could not respond to their people's huge expectations satisfactorily enough after the 1990s collapse of socialist regimes. After a stable and stagnated system, market-driven competition created uncertainty. The promises of greater prosperity did not become established before some political actors had developed populist identifications and mobilisations through antagonism between nationalist authoritarianism and liberal democratic broad-mindedness. However, in some Latin American countries, populism has also served a progressive political identification with civil society. In this context, the political systems are often constituted of a hegemonic and counter-hegemonic dialectic of populist mobilising (e.g. Salojärvi 2016).

In liberal democracies, the consequences of right-wing populism were, according to Mudde and Kaltwasser's (2012b, 212–214) analysis, deeper in national than in communal politics that were controlled by national institutions. The responses to populism also vary. Populist actors may be strongly opposed or isolated by a *cordon sanitaire* as has been done in Sweden and in the Netherlands in the early 21st century, or they can be taken as part of the political field and can be tried to be socialised to the system as in Norway and in Finland. Even in the most critical cultures, other political players have to give up their resistance against populist actors if these become popular and the people's support to their agenda seems strong enough. In Sweden and in Netherlands, for example, the more mainstream parties have started to collaborate with populist radical right actors in issues they have common interests, after stabilisation of populist parties in political field during the late 2010s (see Herkman & Jungar 2021). In more authoritarian contexts the only opposing force for authoritarian rule might paradoxically be another populist movement creating a counter-hegemonic political articulation to the power-bloc (see Palonen 2009; Levitsky & Loxton 2012). Therefore, eventually populism's effect on democracy varies a lot depending on contexts, and no unambiguous answer can be given to the question whether populism is an ultimate treat or a corrective to democracy.

4 Populism and the media

Many scholars agree that the media is essential in the rise and success of populist movements (see Mazzoleni et al. 2003; Mazzoleni 2014; Moffitt 2016). In general, the increasing role of the media in politics has been called mediatisation since the 1990s (Mazzoleni & Schulz 1999). Some scholars argue that a mediated political environment especially supports a populist style because of its appeal to the people. The provocations and salient confrontations match well with the logic of contemporary news media competing fiercely for advertisers', audiences' and public attention (e.g. Esser & Strömbäck 2014; Moffitt & Tormey 2014).

The intensified mutual relationship between politics and media can also be linked to the changes in representative democracies. In the late 20th and early 21st centuries in the Western world, party orientations have diminished and have been transformed into political individualism. In multiparty democracies the status of Prime Ministers has increased, whereas majority parliamentarism has placed the governing cabinets at the centre of the ruling power. In such countries as the United States, France, Russia and Turkey, the status of the Presidency as the leading figure in the country has become even stronger over the last few decades. The political scientist, Bernard Manin (1997), has called this a transformation from party democracy to audience democracy.

According to Manin, the Western world lived the golden age of mass parties from the end of the Second World War to the 1970s. During this era, political parties represented on a large scale societal class structures and the voting behaviour remained enduring. The party identification was strong and based on the feeling that political parties really represented the interests of various social groupings. In party democracy party loyalty was emphasised and voting indicated this confidence to the party. The flip side of stability was the consensus in mass parties that suppressed plurality and the demands of minorities.

DOI: 10.4324/9781003267539-5

Public deliberation remained rather poor, because the most important discussions and decisions were carried out by the inner circles of the parties. However, one can claim that at the general level majority rule was a key feature of party democracy.

During the 1970s, the election studies started to demonstrate that the above-mentioned party democracy was no longer as enduring as it used to be. To maintain their mass popularity in changing societies with an increasing middle class and a structural transformation of work, political parties begun to transform towards the political centre and their ideological differences diminished. The move towards post-industrial societies fractured the class structure and made the traditional left and right division in politics a more unclear basis for political identification than before. At the same time, the media transformed in many countries from being politically and nationally oriented to being a market-driven commercial business in which attraction and entertainment replaced the former ideological underpinnings. The role of the party press started to decline and television took the place as the most important forum of the political public sphere, creating a completely new type of media politician.

In audience democracy, the meaning of a political party gives room to individual politicians and their media appearances as central features of contemporary politics. Media personas are emphasised in politics and also as the leading figures of political parties and governance, because they are highlighted in the news feed. Individual politicians serve as attachment points for political identification, because individual choices have become central in political engagement. Voter volatility increases and voters are more willing to change their candidate than before. Election results become more difficult to predict. Growing individuality increases plurality and minority attention in politics, but at the same time leading politicians start to become estranged from ordinary people and construct a new media controlled elite (Manin 1997, 232).

Obviously societies are different and Manin's theorisation describes better some countries than others. It demonstrates the developments in Western democracies and fits especially into North and Central European multiparty democracies in which a strong welfare state, hegemonic social democratic movements, public service media and political party press faced dramatic challenges during the late 20th and early 21st centuries. The model does not display that well the changes, for example, in Eastern European post-communist democracies or representative democracies in Latin America with long histories of authoritarian regimes.

In their seminal analysis Daniel C. Hallin and Paolo Mancini (2004) called "democratic corporatist" North and Central European countries with an early right to vote and a long history of democracy combined with a strong tendency towards consensual decision-making by various corporations representing interests of different social groups. The media environment in democratic corporatist countries has been equally contradictory, because it has combined highly autonomous and professional media markets with a strong tradition of public service media (Strömbäck et al. 2008; Syvertsen et al. 2014). Other models in Hallin and Mancini's classification represent the "liberal or North Atlantic model", appearing in its purest form in the United States, and the "polarised pluralist or Mediterranean model", common in South European democracies. In the liberal model the tradition of democracy is also as long as in democratic corporatist countries, but political representation and organisations have an individualist and market-driven emphasis that is also promoted in the media systems. In polarised pluralist countries the tradition of democracy is younger and the state regularly intervenes in economics and the media to ensure that they are organised in a pluralist way.

Hallin and Mancini's (2004) models represent system level ideal types rather than particular countries, but in general they link the democratic corporatist model to the Nordic and Benelux countries, Germany, Austria and Switzerland; the liberal model to the United States, the United Kingdom, Ireland and Canada; and the polarised pluralist model to France, Spain, Portugal, Italy and Greece. These three models of politics and media systems therefore represent primarily the traditional Western liberal democracies. More recently Hallin and Mancini (2012) have edited a volume in which a similar system level comparison is proceeded "beyond the Western world" to several other countries. However, the original trisection is also applied in these analyses. For example, in Eastern European post-communist countries the polarised pluralist features of the model have been emphasised, even though country-specific differences and various combinations of models appear.

Hallin and Mancini (2004, 251) concluded their original analysis by claiming that European media systems changed dramatically at the end of the 20th century. During this period the differences between the models decreased and many countries transformed toward the US-style liberal model, meaning weaker public service media, stronger commercial media and general market-driven orientation in media environments. The same is said to be true, for example, even in the Nordic countries, which have previously been thought to maintain most eagerly the public ideal in their media systems (see Skogerbø et al. 2021). In authoritarian countries the political control over the media systems affects the news and information production, although entertainment has often been largely commercialised.

At the same time as transformations have taken place in audience democracies and market-driven media environments, new populist movements have begun to appear in many European democracies. This supports the idea that the crisis in party democracy and spreading of audience democracy are linked to the success of populist movements. The image of politics as a sheer game or show suggested by sensational media publicity means that the domination of media elites is linked to populist articulations between the media and political elite. Simultaneously, the media creates a useful forum for populist provocations and confrontations through which populist antagonisms and identifications can be circulated. Liberal news media face a challenge from nativist right-wing populism, because their basic values confront each other. However, the liberal news media have to report populist actors as part of politics, and populism also interests their audiences and this increases the profit that news media make (Herkman 2016).

Social media in the 21st century have made the situation even more complicated. Henry Jenkins (2008) has used the term "convergence culture" to describe an environment where old and new media collide with each other in numerous and unpredictable ways. In a convergence culture media production and consumption find new forms because of digitalisation and increased networking. Traditional media corporations try to adapt to the situation in which media consumption and users' time is devoted to "free" content sharing and communication on social media platforms. Legacy news media compete with such giant platform and application companies as Google and YouTube, Apple, Facebook and Instagram and Twitter, who dominate todays' media advertising markets.

The logic of social media differs from the logic of traditional mass media and news media (Van Dijck & Poell 2013). Social media allow much more concrete interactivity than traditional mass media, and this is why Internet 2.0 has brought with it high expectations of e-democracy, new communities and transparency, linked to ideas of direct and counter-democracies. Jenkins (2008), for example, has linked his ideas on social media and convergence culture to his previous studies on fan cultures, where he sees a lot of emancipational and political potential. Jenkins writes about "collective intelligence" and "participatory culture" in digitalised and networked activities. Wikipedia is an often mentioned example of these kinds of activities. However, more recently social media algorithms have been criticised for creating "filter bubbles", going well together with intentional misinformation spreading, increased hate speech, trolling and micro-targeted propaganda or political campaignings, even information warfare and making the struggle over politicised meanings in social media platforms very complex processes.

Political actors are usually at the forefront in applying new communication means. The US presidential elections in the 21st century have therefore been called blog, Facebook and Twitter elections in that order, because these platforms were adopted in campaigns as they became increasingly popular among their users. Barack Obama was especially noted for his successful use of YouTube and Facebook in his campaigns (Jenkins 2008), and Donald Trump has become famous for setting news agenda with his tweets during his campaigns and presidency. In convergence culture "old" and "new" media are inherently linked to each other, and topics from news media are spread and commented on in social media and vice versa. Andrew Chadwick (2013) calls this kind of media environment in which political content circulates between different legacy and social media platforms in intensive cycles a "hybrid media system".

Convergence culture creates new borderlines in political communication. Party politics still relies strongly on legacy media, but an increasingly large number of people lives in a convergence culture world in which life politics and civil activism are more popular forms of political activities than institutional party politics. Convergence culture enforced through social media and counter-democracy go hand in hand. There is also a clear generation divide here as well. Even if social media is used by all people, older generations consume remarkably more traditional media forms and legacy media, whereas younger generations spend more of their time on online media and social media platforms. This challenges party politics that still anchors itself to traditional structures in political and media systems.

Therefore, it is not a coincidence that many movements that have been called populist have gained popularity and been mobilised with the help of social media. The success of the Brexit campaign was partly explained by the use of social media in 2016, and in the same year Donald Trump's victory in particular was connected to Facebook communities and his tweets circulating in news media all around the world (see Groshek & Koc-Michalska 2017). Some scholars have argued that especially right-wing populist actors can benefit from social media, because they can use them to bypass news media critique and thus powerfully strengthen their political identifications

(Krämer 2017). It is clear that media in its various forms intertwine in populist identifications and has an inherent role in the rise and success of populist movements.

Mediatisation of politics

Scholars started to talk about the mediatisation of politics in the 1990s when it was clear that media had a great significance for political campaigns, agenda and public opinion (e.g. Mazzoleni & Schulz 1999). Mediatisation theory reflects audience democracy from the perspective of media/politics relationships. Some scholars also discuss mediatisation as a larger phenomenon that penetrates the whole of Western culture, societies and way of life (e.g. Krotz 2007; Hjarvard 2013; Couldry & Hepp 2017). Friedrich Krotz (2007), for example, sees mediatisation as a historical meta-process reminiscent of globalisation, individualisation and commercialisation. However, with regard to politics, mediatisation is defined in narrower way as increasing the impact of media in political institutions and actions (see Esser & Strömbäck 2014).

In English, mediatisation has been separated from mediation, which is an older term that signifies the inter-connectivity or betweenness of subjects (Williams 1988). Mediated communication has referred to indirect forms of communication in anthropology and other social sciences, indicating that something has become a mediator in social interaction (see Sumiala 2013). Therefore, mediatisation (or medialisation) has been used as a more focused term to describe the particular impact of media as an institution and communication technology in various fields of human activity, such as politics, culture or sports (see Thompson 1995; Couldry & Hepp 2017). Mediatisation has also been linked to other narratives of changes such as the professionalisation and Americanisation of political communication, because the increasing impact of media calls for special skills connected to media institutions, and political communication has become increasingly more professionalised following the US model (see Negrine et al. 2007; Stanyer 2007). The spreading of populism in the 21st century has also been inherently linked to the mediatisation of politics (see Mazzoleni 2014).

However, there is no consensus about the forms and depth of political mediatisation among scholars. Some of them have claimed that contemporary politics is totally colonised by the media (e.g. Meyer 2002), others do not recognise such an overriding impact. Jesper Strömbäck (2008) has categorised the mediatisation of politics into four phases to make the process more structured. According to Strömbäck, in the first phase media serve the most important platform for political information. In the second phase media start to operate as a separate institution independent from political institutions. In the third phase the particular media logic starts to guide the operation and content of the media, and in the last phase political institutions begin to follow this media logic. However, scholars remind us that the mediatisation of politics is not a linear process but is instead manifested differently depending on the context. The media/politics relationship is also mutual, thus politics and political institutions also affect the media (Couldry 2008; Esser & Strömbäck 2014). In some liberal democracies that emphasise societal transparency, empirical research has paradoxically shown that the very core of political decision-making tends to hide itself rather than follow the media logic in highly mediated environments (e.g. Vesa 2016).

The four phases of mediatisation are relevant especially in Western liberal democracies. In more authoritarian systems the rulers control the media and mediatisation remains less deep – even though authoritarian leaders also benefit from the media through their strategic communication. However, it is also a matter of debate how deep the mediatisation of politics is in Western democracies. Essential in the mediatisation of politics is two different logics and their relationship, namely media logic and political logic (see Table 4.1). In political logic, practices of policy and politics are essential, and media logic is formed by journalistic criteria and conventions, commercial interests and media and communication technology (Esser & Strömbäck 2014). Sometimes these logics confront each other, because media logic with commercial and watch-dog interests do not necessarily match political logic targeting popularity among voters or political decisions and ruling. Therefore, mediatisation of politics is always context-laden.

Table 4.1 Political and media logics

	Framework	*Goal*	*Operation*
Politics	The institutional and formal framework of politics	Policy and decision-based production of politics	Power- and publicity-gaining presentational politics
News media	Journalistic institutions and media markets, technology	Communications, commercial profit, control of power	News production according to journalistic norms and criteria

Source: Modified from Esser and Strömbäck (2014, 15–19).

The relationship between populism and the media is contradictory (see Moffitt 2016). On the one hand, populism benefits from media attention, on the other hand that attention is often critical in liberal democracies because the values promoted by liberal journalism and especially right-wing populists are confrontational (Herkman 2016; Wettstein et al. 2018). One may even wonder how successful radical right populist movements have been in many Western democracies given the criticism displayed in the mainstream journalistic media. However, it is clear that populist actors do not use journalistic media in their political campaigns in the same way as traditional parties: whereas political parties traditionally try to adapt media logic and thereby apply it in their political communication, populist radical right actors emphasise their antagonism with the media as part of populist identification. In right-wing populist articulation, journalistic media is linked to other societal elite as a hegemonic power-bloc of "them" separated from "us" – "the people" whose opinions these elites do not take into account but instead ignore.

It is also possible to claim that populism highlights the problems in mediatisation theory. Firstly, the mediatisation of politics is anchored to journalism and to the golden era of the mass media. Essential in the mediatisation of politics is the concept of media logic that derives especially from the mass media. However, even if today's party politics is in many countries highly dependent on journalistic news media, it is clear that transformation in the media environment towards convergence culture (Jenkins 2008) or a hybrid media system (Chadwick 2013) has also changed political communication in multiple ways. In the contemporary media environment the community construction is promoted often through digital networks and the significance of the news media as an ultimate agenda controller of public debates has been downsized. One can even argue that the power of the journalistic media and its logic has also more recently diminished in politics. The developments in the media environment have had a specific significance for populism, because populist identifications can now be promoted in social media without news media's control or support.

Secondly, the theory of mediatisation of politics has been focused on Western liberal democracies with strong traditions of party politics and liberal journalistic media. However, populist actors have been successful in countries with remarkably different forms of democracy or media systems in Eastern Europe, Latin America and Asia (cf. Hallin & Mancini 2012). In many of these countries, the role and conditions of the news media is rather different than in Western liberal democracies, and the media might be even totally controlled by authoritarian regimes. In both contexts, social media can serve a forum for anti-hegemonic counter-voices, but it works in a completely opposite way in authoritarian countries as a forum for progressive liberal opposition than in liberal democracies, where it serves a platform for conservative and nativist voices challenging the liberal hegemony (Herkman & Matikainen 2016).

Media populism

Some scholars argue that commercial media is itself often populist and refer to this as media populism (Krämer 2014, 42; Mazzoleni 2014, 47–48). Media populism refers first and foremost to media's commercial interest in selling its content to audiences and advertisers and this leads to populist methods, namely dramatisation with strong antagonisms, highlighting individual experiences rather than social structures or objective facts, adopting the people's point of view and attacking the elite. Media are also keen to appeal to morality and arouse emotions, because sensational headlines, scandals and click journalism awake audience interest and fit well into the media's commercial aims.

Etymologically the words popular and populism derive from the same Latin word populus, meaning the people (see Krämer 2014, 51; Williams 1988, 237–238). As such, populist logic is rather reminiscent of the commercial logic of the popular media. Populist identification is based on strong antagonisms and a provocative style from which media can draw material that is of interest to audiences and advertisers. Populism creates political drama that news media demand. It is no secret that Donald Trump was an economic lucky stroke for the US news media that had suffered for several decades from shrinking business: Trump's provocations and sensations increased their audience and advertiser attention remarkably (Borchers 2016). In addition, the watch-dog ideal associated with liberal journalism also fits media populism, because it carries an elite-critical undertone reminiscent of populism (Esser et al. 2017).

Another dimension in media populism might therefore be that journalism adopts the agendas and perspectives of populist actors. This has been linked especially to so-called tabloid media that tends to identify itself as popular and anti-elitist (e.g. Fiske 1992). There are studies that support this claim. For example, in Finland and Norway the tabloid press seems to be more sympathetic to domestic radical right populist actors than legacy media (Herkman 2017b), and the Austrian FPÖ gained remarkable support from domestic tabloid media during the 2000s (Plasser & Ultram 2003; Wodak 2013). A recent comparison in ten European countries found that in general news media evaluated populist actors negatively but the media presented themselves often as a proponent of the people and as critical towards institutionalised politicians and parties. This was especially true in tabloid media that largely represented this kind of media populist attitude (Wettstein et al. 2018). However, not all studies support the difference between the tabloid and legacy media (e.g. Akkerman 2011; Bos et al. 2011). Gianpierto Mazzoleni (2014, 51) reminds us that there are significant differences between countries and political contexts. Even if tabloids seem to be more sympathetic towards populist actors in Anglo-American context, the nativist Sweden Democrats, for example, has been evaluated very negatively also in Swedish tabloid media, because the party has been excluded from political agenda-setting by a common *cordon sanitaire* in Sweden (Rydgren 2010; Herkman 2017b; Wettstein et al. 2018).

Therefore, the relationship between journalistic news media and populism in Western democracies is twofold. On the one hand, media can benefit from the dramatic content that populism creates for political newsfeed and simultaneously provides visibility to populist actors and their agendas. On the other hand, liberal journalism confronts populism that promotes contradictory views on its basic values of equality and minority rights. Because especially right-wing populism leans on exclusive majority rule, liberal journalism is critical of radical right actors and their approaches (see Wettstein et al. 2018).

However, the collision between populism and liberal news media does not necessarily decrease their popularity. On the contrary, as has discussed earlier, the political drama displayed by populist actors is interesting and good for media business, and populist actors can link news media to their ultimate enemy, the corrupt societal elite, as part of their populist identifications. In fact, the criticism in news media may even increase the popularity of a populist movement, since it affectively accelerates its supporters' group identification especially in the early mobilisation phase of the movement. The leaders of populist movements often play the underdogs of the journalistic media, rousing anger against the media and sympathy towards the "victim" among their supporters (Mazzoleni et al. 2003). Populist actors may also push the news agenda towards topics that are important for them, such as immigration, crime and corruption of the elite, and represent themselves as experts in these topics rather than as pure political challengers (Walgrave & De Swert 2004).

Some scholars argue that populist actors intentionally exploit the sensitivity of liberal news media in their strategic communication by deliberately provoking "sensationalist" content to the media (e.g. Stewart et al. 2003; Mazzoleni 2014; Wodak 2015). Former reality-TV billionaire Donald Trump has fed the newsfeed continuously before and during his presidency by his tweets, and Austrian Freedom Party FPÖ succeeded in controlling media attention strategically with various public sensations and scandals during the 2000s (Wodak 2013). The critical discourse analyst Ruth Wodak (2015) has called this the "right-wing populist perpetuum mobile", the circulation of populist agendas in public discussion through intentional provocations. This communication strategy puts the liberal news media in an awkward position, because it should inform citizens about interesting and important political issues and give voice to different political perspectives but, at the same time, its ideals encourage defending the core values of liberal democracy from violent attacks from radical right actors.

Perhaps most salient is the tension between political and media populism in political scandals linked to populist actors. Especially right-wing populists have faced several public scandals in liberal democracies, because they openly attack and slight various minorities, immigrants, multi-culturalism and Islam. The former leader of the FPÖ, Jörg Haider (1950–2008), for example, was involved in several public scandals because of his anti-Semitic provocations in the early 21st century, and the leader of the Dutch Party for Freedom (PVV), Geert Wilders, caused an international scandal in 2007 by comparing *the Quran* to Adolf Hitler's *Mein Kampf*. In the same year, one of the leading figures of the Danish People's Party (DF), Morten Messerschmidt, caused a scandalous fuss because he was claimed to sing Nazi songs and make a Nazi salute in Copenhagen's Tivoli. Messerschmidt won the court case based on the scandal in 2009. Nevertheless, the same kinds of public scandals have been witnessed in almost all Western democracies with well-known right-wing populist actors during the 21st century (see Herkman & Matikainen 2019).

The British sociologist, John B. Thompson (2000, 120–123), has found three main types of political scandals: sex, power and money scandals. However, Thompson's classification does not cover well scandals linked to contemporary populist politicians, because traditional political scandals are connected to political elites from whom populists distance themselves. In fact, traditional political scandals are used in populist identifications as tools for antagonism because, according to populists, they prove the alleged corruption of the political elite. However, the Nordic media scholars, Sigurd Allern and Ester Pollack (2016, 157), have demonstrated in their studies that particularly scandals deriving from politicians' inappropriate behaviour or talk have increased in the Nordic countries during the 21st century. Most of these scandals can be explained by the increasing support of right-wing populist actors and sensations linked to them in the Nordic region (Herkman 2018).

Scandals linked to right-wing populist actors often start from their insulting statements against immigrants or other minorities – commonly made in social media forums. In some cases right-wing populists flirt with more radical extreme right actors or even sympathise with Nazism. Sometimes commentators are drunk or their statements are made by accident, but usually comments are given on purpose to restricted audiences from which they spread or are leaked to other forums on purpose. The liberal news media starts to circulate and criticise the norm-transgression largely in the public sphere, but the populist actor accused of making insults and norm-transgression generally denies the action and plays the role of the victim of a media witch hunt. Characteristically, his or her supporters mobilise a counter-campaign in the social media in which the accused is defended and the media blamed. Depending on the case, the scandal ends in a juridical or political sanction, but this does not affect the popularity of the populist actor, whose supporters think that those who judged him or her represent a corrupt elite. On the contrary, the scandal may even strengthen the populist identification of the supporters (Herkman 2018).

According to a comparative analysis of populist communication, right-wing populist movements have to balance between radical and more moderate voices in public discussions after being successful in elections (Hatakka et al. 2017). On the one hand, they have to continue to appeal to their radical supporters by using strong confrontational rhetoric against liberal politicians, news media and immigrants on the other hand, they have to show to their less radical voters that they can act in an appropriate way in political institutions. The radical rhetoric is more common in social media and is promoted by particular members of the parties, but leading figures in the party usually appear to be more moderate in mainstream publicity. However, there are exceptions such as Donald Trump and Jair Bolsonaro, who continued their radical and scandalous statements after being elected as presidents. Both radical and moderate rhetoric is also used in news media comments in which parties respond to, for example, accusations of racism. Typical to radical populist parties is a double-speech strategy in which a large audience is addressed moderately through the mainstream media and the core community is addressed with backstage tough talks (Mudde 2000, 168–169). This, of course, makes public scandals possible if backstage commentaries are revealed in mainstream publicity.

Life-cycle model

The relationship between populism and the media depends on political culture, the media system and the status of political populist actors in particular contexts. In Latin American politics, populism has been a structural element of many political systems (see Salojärvi 2016), but in Western democracies populist movements have often been seen as momentary exceptions (e.g. Wiles 1969; Taggart 2000). Also in the Western liberal media, populist styles have been regarded as a sort of special case among political discourse, but in some South-American countries populist styles have been a publicly accepted form of political communication (e.g. Hennessy 1969; Levitsky & Loxton 2012).

Gianpietro Mazzoleni et al. (2003) studied the relationship of media and populism in several European countries at the beginning of the 2000s. They concluded their comparative study with a life-cycle model showing the correlation between media attention and the development of new populist movements (see Table 4.2). Despite some contextual differences, they found four major phases in the media's relationship with all neo-populist movements: "the ground-laying", "the insurgent", "the established" and "the decline" phases (Stewart et al. 2003, 219–224; also Mazzoleni 2008, 59–62). Essential to the life-cycle model was also the division between the two main types of news media, namely "elite" and "tabloid" media, suggesting that the former is more mainstream and supports the political *status quo* of the traditional parties, whereas the latter thrives on sensationalism, scandal and social and moral anxieties to attract mass audiences.

Table 4.2 Life-cycle of a neo-populist movement

Life phase	*Timing in life-cycle*	*Media attention*	*Tabloid media*	*Elite media*
A ground-laying phase	Before the movement breaks	Media creates anti-politics atmosphere	Politics critical	Politics critical
An insurgent phase	A breakthrough of the movement	Great	Complying with the movement	Critical against the movement
An established phase	Establishing of the movement	Diminishing, normalising	Turns critical against the movement	Neutral news about the movement
A decline phase	The movement fades away	Minor or non-existent	Stops discussing the movement	Stops discussing the movement

Source: Stewart et al. (2003, 219–224).

The ground-laying phase is characterised by social and political discontent in a country, during which the media tends to create a political climate engendering populist discourse and sentiment, for example, by trivialising and personalising political issues. According to the life-cycle model there is no significant difference between the media types during the ground-laying phase since both "contribute to the diffusion of populist discourse" (Stewart et al. 2003, 219–220).

The insurgent phase is characterised by intense media attention on populist movements because the messages, appearances and rhetoric they promote nurture the journalistic and commercial logic of the media. In general, the tabloid media promotes a more populist discourse, whereas the elite media applies a critical distance (ibid. 221–222). However, the elite media "soften" their policies if they are in danger of losing some of their audience. Both ground-laying and insurgent phases take place during the early growth of populist movements.

In the established phase, the populist movement achieves some legitimacy and status as a national political player, but its share of attention in the media usually shrinks. As Mazzoleni (2008, 61) states, this is a critical phase for populist movements, who tend to become disenchanted, especially with the tabloid media, after achieving public legitimisation within politics. However, the elite media will often be forced to report on and discuss populist issues because it has to take the populists seriously once they have become established. Nevertheless, if the populist movement really challenges the political *status quo* and social order, most media, especially elite media, will try to strengthen support for the ruling political parties through hostile coverage of the populists (Stewart et al. 2003, 222–223).

The decline phase refers to the fading of the populist movement from the media, although not all movements are faced with this phase and may gain new success. Thus, media attention varies from country to country depending on the newsworthiness of the demise of the movement, or whether, for example, a new populist movement arises from the ashes of a former movement (ibid. 223–224). However, Mazzoleni (2008, 61–62) has pointed out that this phase is not relevant to many European populist movements because they "are still fairly successful and continue to receive significant media attention". The context of the 21st century seems to create fertile soil for the blossoming of right-wing populist parties that have created in Europe a new rather established and enduring party type (Zaslove 2008).

In general, the media pays significant attention to populist actors as part of political news feed, but this attention is rather negative at least towards right-wing populist approaches whose agenda confronts the basic values of liberal journalism (Herkman 2016; Wettstein et al. 2018). Therefore, the mainstreaming of populist parties may be better portrayed by some other theories of normalisation than the life-cycle model (see Adams et al. 2004; Horowitz & Browne 2004). The development of these parties can be discussed, for example, with the help of Giovanni Sartori's (2005 [1976]) classic description of "the anti-system party" transformation towards "the pro-system party", in which the Sweden Democrats (SD) is a typical example: SD was established by neo-Nazis in 1988, but especially the current party leader, Jimmie Åkesson (2005–), has transformed SD by building up a nationwide party organisation and distancing the party from its past with the aim of developing a more electorally attractive party with governing potential (Herkman & Jungar 2021). Similarly, James Shields (2014) has analysed how the French radical right party the National Front (National Rally since 2018) has systematically tried to be normalised as a legitimate government party under the leadership of Marine Le Pen, and the same kind of process has been followed in many European countries.

However, as Shields (2014, 499) argues, the problem with this kind of perspective is that parties often include contradictory elements, meaning that they may be normalised in their party system with some elements but still remain "radical" with others. Tjitske Akkerman (2016), for example, demonstrated with her colleagues in their large-scale comparative analysis that European radical right parties have not been "softened" but remained radical in their approaches to immigration and nationalism, even if they have gained rather established positions in their domestic party systems, as well as at the European level.

One dimension in the normalising of populist radical right parties is their possible influence on other parties or even on the general political discourse. Thus, these parties might become more normal in their party fields through transformation in their political environments rather than in the parties themselves. Céline Leconte (2015), for example, has demonstrated how Euroscepticism – promoted first mainly by peripheral populist parties – has become a mainstream and enduring phenomenon in several European democracies, and Giorel Curran (2004) has indicated likewise that right-wing populist parties in Italy and Australia had succeeded in injecting their "populist" themes and "prejudices" regarding leadership and criticism of immigration into the mainstream political discourse by the early 2000s. In Denmark, the party field has turned rather positive to nationalist and nativist themes promoted first only by Danish People's Party during the 2000s (Herkman & Jungar 2021).

It is evident that the role of media has been essential in these processes. Matt Guardino and Dean Snyder (2012) argue, for example, that the corporate news media played a central role in mainstreaming right-wing populist discourse represented by the Tea Party in the aftermath of the US 2008 financial crisis and economic recession. According to their analysis, both conservative (FOX) and liberal (CNN) television networks framed the movement positively. More recently, this situation has changed with regard to Donald Trump, but one may claim that the mainstreaming of the Tea Party's discourse may have created fertile ground for Trump's success in the 2016 presidential elections, promoted thereafter especially on social media platforms and accompanied by an increasing confrontation between conservative and liberal news media. Trump has even repeated the same slogans familiar from the Tea Party.

Despite certain problems with the life-cycle model, it serves an interesting approach to media/populism relationships and displays quite aptly the early phases in the developments of populist movements. It is clear that there are significant differences between countries, but several studies have indicated a correlation between media attention and the increasing success of these movements (e.g. Boomgaarden & Vliegenthart 2007; Bos et al. 2011; Roodjuin 2014; Herkman 2017b). However, the main problem in the life-cycle model is that it is based on an "old media system" in which the mass media dominates. Since that, the media environment has been radically transformed by digitalisation and networkisation, remarkably changing also populism/media relationships. The social media in particular have changed the practices of political communication and served as the most important forum for populist identifications. Therefore, it is impossible today to consider populism or the mediatisation of politics without taking into account the huge impact of social media.

Social media and populism

Social media has significantly changed the political communication environment since the beginning of the millennium. However, there are quite conflicting views on the impact of social media on politics. On the one hand, some believe that politics has been completely revolutionised by the influence of social media (e.g. Jenkins 2008). On the other hand, several empirical studies have shown that in most Western countries the role of the Internet and social media in election results has remained relatively modest and television was still the central media during the 2000s. However, research nearer the end of 2010s demonstrates the constantly consolidating and increasing importance of social media in various areas of political communication. For example, the results of the 2016 US presidential election and the UK Brexit vote show, according to many analyses, the great importance of social media in these campaigns (e.g. Groshek & Koc-Michalska 2017), and increasing micro-targeted campaigning, rallying and trolling in social media has more recently led to public debates about the possible impact of social media on democracies as whole.

On the one hand, the political system maintains permanence and is slow to change: political institutions and practices, at least in stabile democracies, do not change in an instant. Leading politicians therefore value traditional means of communication, such as the major news media. They also help to reach the widest possible audience, and news media play an important role as a feed and target for social media content. In a hybrid media environment, policy news circulate from traditional media to the online environment and vice versa (Chadwick 2013, 62–63). On the other hand, politicians are often among the first to adopt new means of communication because, in a professionalised political communication environment, they are encouraged and educated to do so. It is also important for politicians, especially in the campaigning phase, to reach the widest possible audience, and here the use of fresh means of communication serve as an excellent extension to the old forums.

The strong connection of party politics to the traditional mainstream media produces segregation in the political field. Among those who have grown up in a convergence culture, politics based on institutions may be perceived as foreign. For them, the familiarity of social media, strong confrontations, strong communality and the simultaneous pursuit of individual interests are typical starting points for political action (Jenkins 2008). As a result, a large number of those who are tired of or are disenchanted with party politics direct their political interest to social media channels. This also provides opportunities for populist movements that challenge the hegemony of the ruling parties through social media by confronting both the politicians in power and the journalistic media by claiming that they have forgotten the will of the ordinary people (Bartlett et al. 2011). Especially in liberal democracies, the importance of social media may thus be much more pronounced for populist actors than for ruling parties – at least in the early stages of the life-cycle of populist movements as they grow in popularity.

Some scholars have linked online communication and social media inherently to populism, as populists favour the direct connection to the "people" and appreciate the opportunities that online communication creates for making rude comments. The "attention economy" of online communication sits very well with a populist style with attributes such as drama, confrontation, moralism, straightforwardness, ordinariness and offensive language use (Engesser et al. 2017, 1285–1286). Some of these means also describe, for example, the media populism of the tabloid media, but the simplicity of the populist style, appealing to emotions and negativity are particularly well-suited to the Internet and social media forums that favour maximising attention through such means (see Table 4.3). It can also be argued that social media provide an excellent channel for strengthening populist identifications and mobilisations because there are no real barriers to such activities on social media, and the algorithms of the platforms actually support these processes.

The logic of social media is based on the pursuit of popularity and connectivity (Van Dijck & Poell 2013). The confrontations between native inhabitants and those from elsewhere, especially made by radical right-wing populists, have benefitted from the new media environment, as people are quite free to express escalating and hostile opinions and build their own like-minded community online (e.g. Krämer 2017). The algorithms of social media applications may also strengthen the nativist filter bubbles by guiding users who are favouring similar content.

However, community building is not completely inconsistent even in social media bubbles. For example, more radical and moderate views may clash with like-minded groups and proponents of the most extreme ideas believe that right-wing populist parties that have established themselves in a democracy are often too weak in their demands for immigration policies, for example (see Hatakka 2017). This results in the aforementioned "double speech", in which a more radical language can be used in one's own group than in public. Contradictions

Table 4.3 Logics of populism and social media

	Framework for action	*The core of the operation*	*Target*
Populism	Civil society, political system	Antagonistic identity building, politicisation	Gaining power, challenging hegemony
Social media	Internet, social community services	Online communication, affective experiences	Getting attention, building connections

in social media communities also emphasise the importance of the opinion leaders in the same way as in any communicative communities. Thus, who says what also matters in populist communication and highlights the importance of the leading figures. For example, making populist accusations against some other actors – politicians, immigrants – may even mean that accusers themselves become the subject of criticism if they do not enjoy great confidence among supporters of the ideas (see Hameleers & Schmuck 2017).

At least five ways to exploit social media populistically have been found (see Engesser et al. 2017): First, social media makes it easy to constitute the idea of people's sovereignty. Second, anyone can present themselves as the spokesman of the "forgotten people" on social media. Third, campaigns against various elites can also be successfully built on social media because that is where campaigns quickly find their way. Fourth, and perhaps the most salient claim, is that social media allow for the sharpest criticism and exclusion of other groups of people. Fifth, it is easy to produce cohesion on social media by building one's own idea of a "heartland", a common shared past and a lost land of milk and honey. This is because whereas legacy media are permeated by the logic of professionally produced journalism and relatively passive audiences, social media are characterised by a "network logic" with a focus on forming like-minded networks of friends (Van Dijck & Poell 2013; Klinger & Svensson 2015).

According to a comparative study in Western democracies, of the above-mentioned populist uses of social media, opposition to the elite in particular and acting as the proponent of the people have been most common (Ernst et al. 2017). The same study found that populist communication on social media was primarily practised by political actors at ideological extremes. In the party field, the populist use of social media was significantly more common among the opposition than among the governing parties. Social media thus generally serve as a channel for challenging hegemonic power. However, there are significant country-specific differences here, stemming from contextual differences in the political system, power relations and the media environment. For example, the above-mentioned study found that Facebook fits better in populist communication than Twitter, because in many countries Twitter serves as an information channel of the elite such as experts, leading politicians, journalists and cultural figures. However, in Switzerland and the United States, for example, Twitter has also been used very successfully for populist opinion-forming in the 2010s elections and politics. In Latin America, left-wing populists have harnessed Twitter for one-way communication, in which they sharply oppose the criticism of them by citizens, the media or political rivals (Waisbord & Amado 2017).

Indeed, many populist actors know how to use social media skilfully to express their own ideas and provoke the news media, of which Donald Trump is probably a prime example. The activities of the Austrian Freedom Party FPÖ, for example, have also been analysed from this perspective (see Wodak 2013). Such populist actors take advantage of the "right-wing populist perpetuum mobile", as Wodak puts it (2013; 2015), in which actors deliberately and repeatedly provoke the liberal journalistic media with their cutting-edge claims and thus garner constant media attention. Even if this attention is negative for populist actors, it can still direct the public agenda to the topics they want. From the point of view of their supporters, the criticality of the news media serves in their eyes as evidence that the mainstream media are part of a corrupt elite trying to silence the voice of their representative and the forgotten people.

Populist actors may also make provocative outputs through traditional news media, but social media in particular provide a forum for community building that can bring together supporters of more radical and moderate political movements. For example, supporters of the Alternative für Deutschland (AfD) party, which has been a publicly accepted German party, and Pediga, which is grouped as a far right movement, form a reasonably convergent audience on social media forums, although support for the movements is otherwise quite differentiated (Stier et al. 2017). This is explained by the fact that other ruling parties form a strong consensus-minded counterpart that opposes the anti-immigration views of both movements. A similar situation has existed in Sweden, where the Sweden Democrats Party has grown in popularity as other political actors have excluded the party from debate and decision-making. According to populist logic, a strong consensus feeds a confrontation in which populists get to challenge hegemonic power as an intact cartel, and this challenging takes often place on social media forums.

There has also been a lot of discussion in the 2010s about strategic online spin strategies for example in elections where foreign states or other "third parties" can campaign to support a candidate or try to create general confusion in the political field by means of social media. Social media have become perhaps the most central tool of modern propaganda, as they allow communication to be precisely targeted to desired groups without journalistic control. The public has discussed, among other things, Russian-influenced online advocacy attempts in European and US politics. In this so-called information warfare, populist movements often act as intermediaries that foreign powers want to support, because the success of populists causes confusion in national party fields and undermines the unity and capacity of European and American political actors at the international level. Some radical right parties in Europe (including Hungary and Greece) have also expressed their sympathy for Putin-led Russia and received Russian funding for their activities.

Therefore, the different connections between populism and social media highlight the changes that have taken place in the field of political communication. These changes constitute a hybrid media system in which traditional professionally produced news media and user-driven social media are intertwined in multiple ways (Chadwick 2013). Depending on the national political and media systems, these connections take different forms. In liberal democracies, social media is often used populistically to confront the hegemonic position of the ruling parties and the journalistic media. In more authoritarian systems, social media often serve as a forum for liberal opposition because the populist movement has gained hegemonic power and subjugated journalistic media to become its own mouthpiece (Herkman & Matikainen 2016). In both cases, the ideas of "collective intelligence" or "participatory culture" (see Jenkins 2008) seem far-fetched ideals rather than real progressive means of politics. Instead of utopias, the social media have become part of the reality of political communication and mobilisation, where all means are taken to promote a political message – for better or worse.

5 Three perspectives on populism

Populism as a process and phenomenon draws its strength from political and economic crises, but its forms vary according to the local cultural and political contexts. The problems of party politics are always national problems, thus political crises are different and create varying contexts for the rise of populism. The context, in turn, determines which confrontations, enemies and ideologies at any given time provide the best combination to construct the identity of a forgotten people and appeal most widely to the supporters of populist actors. In other words, populist identifications are always determined contingently within the framework of each historical moment and circumstance, which explains the multi-faceted and local nature of populism (see Laclau 1977; Laclau 2005).

However, it is clear that broader historical currents or conjunctures, such as economic and geopolitical cycles, also frame the local contexts from which populism draws its political resources (Murdock 2020). For example, earlier in the chapter commenting history of populism, the significance of urbanisation, industrialisation and the development of modernisation as backgrounds for various historical forms of populism were presented. This chapter discusses three broader phenomena or concepts that can be argued to frame the new populism prevalent in the late 20th and early 21st century, especially in Europe but also elsewhere. These are the welfare state, globalisation and postmodernism, of which the idea of the welfare state in particular is quite European- and Western-centred, but globalisation in particular can be considered central to new populism regardless of the continent or the form of government (see Hadiz & Chryssogelos 2017).

The welfare state, globalisation and postmodernism are all concepts whose meanings and contents have been the subject of lively academic debate and whose implications have been extensively and empirically studied. They are also politically charged terms used to justify

DOI: 10.4324/9781003267539-6

political decisions and campaigns. Populism itself has contributed to the politicisation of these concepts, as new populism can in many ways be said to be a reaction to the challenges posed to the welfare state by globalisation and postmodernism. This applies above all to Western liberal democracies, so the structure of this chapter illuminates the frameworks of populism, especially in this limited context.

The three concepts describe different dimensions or levels of changing reality. The welfare state is a concrete phenomenon related to the organisation of society, people's living conditions, the economy and policy-making. Globalisation, on the other hand, is a more abstract, transnational phenomenon and is a concept that describes megatrends in the economy and in politics since the late 20th century. Postmodernism, in turn, refers on an even more abstract level to some kind of "Zeitgeist" or mentality shift that radiates, especially at the level of culture – symbols, meanings – to our ways of understanding ourselves, others and reality resonating especially with the cultural approach to populism. I will next consider populism using these three concepts in the above order, because I believe that such a structured movement from the specific to the general illustrates well the contextual determinants that have made the contemporary political environment favourable to populism.

Welfare state

After the Second World War, the world and Europe in particular split in two: into the socialist East and the Western "free world". In the Eastern Bloc, the state began to control virtually all forms of activities, whereas the West relied on the free market economy. However, the world wars had also affected the Western world of values in such a way that the role of the state was seen as important. There was a desire to build mechanisms to prevent the development of a similar devastation as that which resulted from two world wars in the first half of the 20th century. Strengthening constitutional-based liberal democracies was one way of trying to secure equal civil rights for all, regardless of social status, wealth or worldview. To defend human rights and equality, the United Nations (UN) was set up with the task of involving states worldwide in these goals and building a platform for interaction so that crises between the states did not escalate into disasters like the Second World War (Hobsbawm 1994).

A popular position in the economy was given to the British economist John Maynard Keynes (1883–1946), who encouraged states to promote active financial policies. According to Keynes, the state should pursue investments because they would keep the economy running and the unemployment number reasonable, even if the free market deteriorated. Indeed, the role of the public sector and the state as a financial actor that balanced economic cycles and safeguarded the well-being of citizens began to be strengthened in the West in the 1950s (Hobsbawm 1994). The idea of a welfare state originated in Britain, where it was believed that the collapse of the middle class had enabled the rise of the Nazi regime in 1930s Germany, and the welfare state would help to ensure that this would not happen again. An active social policy was planned to build a safety net that would prevent a similar collapse. Many other countries also adopted the idea of a welfare state, which received slightly different emphases depending on the country. In the Nordic countries, the role of the welfare state has been seen as perhaps most important and has been sustained largely with the help of tax revenues collected by the state. In the Anglo-American environment, there has been a desire to keep taxation low and to emphasise individual freedoms, and in Central Europe, welfare services have been largely financed by insurance contributions (Esping-Anderssen 1999).

Politically, the construction of the welfare state was associated with the strengthening of the social democratic movement in many countries. Social Democratic parties thrived, especially in the 1960s and 1970s, which were also the golden age of the idea of the welfare state. The power of the Social Democrats and the idea of a welfare state succeeded most prominently in Sweden, where the Social Democratic Party ruled for nearly 40 years from the 1930s to the late 1970s and built the idea of all citizens uniting to form a "folkhem" (people's home). In many other countries, the popularity of the Social Democrats was less prevalent, although the idea of the welfare state received strong support everywhere in Western Europe and levelled people's living conditions and social security.

At the same time as the construction of welfare states, populist movements emerged protesting against a strong state and strong taxation. Whereas in Sweden the idea of a "folkhem" was so pervasive that it did not produce any outspoken opposition, populist tax protest movements arose in other Nordic countries. For example, the progress parties established in Denmark and Norway in the early 1970s were initially clear tax revolt movements that opposed the strong role of the state and high taxation (Jungar 2017). The Finnish Rural Party (SMP), founded in Finland as early as 1959, succumbed more to the changes caused by rapid urbanisation and industrialisation and thus represented the agrarian-populist resistance caused by structural transformation in society, but in the 1960s and 1970s it also included opposition to "corrupt white-collar offenders" and taxation. The earlier wave of 20th-century populism was thus partly related to the growth pains of the welfare state and, for example, the exclusion of non-native inhabitants on ethnic grounds was not an essential part of that populism. Compared to contemporary right-wing populist parties, the popularity of these movements often remained relatively low with some local exceptions, such as the Finnish Rural Party in the early 1980s.

However, the trends in economic policy began to reverse in the 1970s, when accumulation of capital led to a period of long-term unemployment and rising inflation, further raising taxes and social security costs in many Western countries. The market produced new economic apostles, such as Friedrich von Hayek (1899–1992) and Milton Friedman (1912–2006), who fought against Keynesian economic policies and state intervention. A trend called neoliberalism relied on a monetarist economic policy in which central banks, separate from the state, regulated inflation by their supplies of money (Harvey 2005). The new economic doctrine challenged the idea of a welfare state, because without an active economic state policy, it is difficult to maintain the functions and funding of the welfare state. Neoliberalism began to be more prominent in many Western democracies in the 1980s. At the same time, Social Democratic movements and the left in general lost their positions in the political fields when the middle classes raised by the welfare states strengthened and the left's message no longer spoke to the population to the same extent as before, and political parties began to turn towards the centre in their ideologies (Manin 1997).

Instead of the unease about the welfare state, concerns now began to be raised in the 1980s about the competitiveness of states, which meant tax reliefs, cuts in social security and increased flexibility in the labour market. Sociologists spoke of the transition from a state-based planned economy to a market-based competitive economy, where the state should produce the most effective conditions for succeeding in economic competition (Cerny 1997; Jessop 2002). The main target for a competitive state is therefore to succeed in the global market. The financial policy consequences of increasing competitiveness have been lower income tax progression, austerity measures in state funding and redirection of state subsidies into businesses. Together, these measures have weakened the equality of citizens and the equalisation of income distribution, which was at the heart of the welfare state, and increased income disparities, which is at the heart of the competitive state

(Harvey 2005). At the same time, the number of disadvantaged people has increased in many countries and the state's ability to take care of them has weakened. The idea of a competitive state finally permeated after the new recession experienced in many Western democracies in the early 1990s, when it was realised that the cost of maintaining a welfare state exceeded the financial capacity of national economies.

However, the idea of the welfare state has remained very popular among citizens in Europe, despite the widespread competitive state policy pursued over the last few decades. At the end of the 20th century, equal access to education, access to health and medical services and social security became more self-evident in Western democracies, which citizens value and want to hold on to. The populist uprisings against taxes of the 1970s subsided when people realised the benefits of the welfare state and accepted it as their core value. Most political parties in the Nordic countries, for example, have usually flagged their support for the welfare state in their election campaigns, because these policies enjoy such widespread support among voters that opposing them is not a successful election ploy. At the same time, however, the different types of government parties have pursued pro-competitive economic policies that erode the idea of a strong welfare state.

The contradiction between the politics pursued and the heavy welfare net expectations of citizens has contributed to the rise of populist movements that criticise the ruling parties in many Western democracies. Voters have been puzzled when parties, regardless of their political underpinnings, have implemented neoliberal policies once they have come to power, eroding the base of the welfare services. In the hegemony of competitive state ideology, there do not seem to be genuine political options, meaning that voters become frustrated, voting activity and party participation weaken and the number of floating voters increases. In a situation like this, it is easy for populist movements to build confrontations with the parties in power and promise change in policy. In the eyes of many voters, populists may seem to be the only real option when other parties have so unanimously adopted the idea of a competitive state and a neoliberal ethos.

The attitude of populist movements towards the welfare state demonstrates the multi-faceted nature of populism. For example, nationalist right-wing populists cannot usually directly oppose the welfare state because then they would not receive widespread support in elections. Their response to the crisis in the welfare state, thus, is "welfare chauvinism". This means that most right-wing populists argue that welfare services should be guaranteed first and foremost for native inhabitants, and immigrants should not be granted such benefits to the same extent (see Bay et al. 2013). On the other hand, talking about the political right may even be misleading in the context of some nativist populist movements, as their economic emphasis is more to the left on the traditional ideological map than to the right. For example, the Sweden Democrats are strongly anchored in the Social Democratic ideal of "folkhem", even though the party's background is in National Socialist extremism (Herkman & Jungar 2021).

There are of course significant contextual differences in this. For example, Donald Trump's authoritarian populism in the United States in the 2010s and 2020s united groups that oppose the state interventions and fear that welfare state means "communist" threat to their individual freedom resembling populist tax-protest movements in the early 1970s (see Norris & Inglehart 2019). The ideological flexibility of populism makes these kinds of differences in regard to welfare state possible. Many right-wing populist leaders represent themselves as proponents of ordinary or even underprivileged people, even if their economic policies support big business. Populism can, where appropriate, link either left- or right-wing economic views to other key signifiers, such as nativist opposition to immigrants or criticism of international business giants. The erosion of the welfare state can thus be seen as a frame of reference within which the current Western populist actors articulate their political demands in various ways.

Globalisation

Because globalisation has, according to many interpretations, meant a reduction in the political influence of nation states and an increase in the power of supranational markets, economies and political actors, some of the challenges the welfare state faces are related to it. The welfare state has been seen primarily as a nation state-related project. Welfare states are largely funded by national taxes or other nationally organised solutions. Thus, it is understandable that if decision-making in these matters is seen to be narrowed at the national level or transferred to supranational actors, the welfare state will face difficulties. The problems of the welfare state are closely related to the challenges posed to nation states by neoliberal economic globalisation, which have encouraged states to compete with each other, for example, in taxation and labour costs (see Hadiz & Chryssogelos 2017).

At its simplest, globalisation refers to the increase in intercontinental interaction in different areas of human activity, such as the economy, culture and politics (Held & McGrew 2002). Thus, globalisation extends the human activity traditionally organised within nation states to between nations and even continents. However, there are quite different interpretations of the main dimensions, history and consequences of globalisation. Some scholars emphasise the economic aspects of globalisation, for others cultural or political dimensions of globalisation, for example, are even more central. It is often agreed that the era of globalisation began in the late 20th century, but some scholars point out that the world has been "global" even before that. For some, globalisation means a better world, a more widespread distribution of welfare to humankind and the strengthening of peaceful coexistence; for others it means increased inequality and exploitation, ecological destruction, the loss of biodiversity or the erosion of the welfare state. As such, globalisation is an empty or floating signifier that can be filled with different meanings and can be used for very different political or research purposes (see Ampuja 2012).

Most commonly, globalisation is associated with the economy. Economic globalisation means the greater movement of capital, financial flows, products and labour across the borders of nation states and continents. This also means that national economies are highly dependent on global markets. Supranational economic cycles are shaking national economies whose currencies are floating and in which multinational corporations play a key role in business. In such a "global economy", crises in distant places often have repercussions on national economies, which is why various mechanisms and institutions have been built to regulate and balance markets, both globally and regionally. Examples of these are the World Trade Organization (WTO), the World Monetary Fund (IMF), G7 and G8 meetings and the European, Asian and North and Latin American Market Areas (Held & McGrew 2002).

Many economists see economic globalisation as good and desirable. In their view, a free global market is the best way to enable cost-effective production, overall economic growth and, ultimately, the spread of prosperity worldwide. However, critics of economic globalisation point out that welfare is not in fact evenly distributed as large corporations seek the cheapest possible production costs. The world, moreover, is divided into prosperous societies in the Northern hemisphere and mainly developing countries in the Southern hemisphere that produce raw materials and cheap commodities for the North. The location of production to low-cost countries often also has detrimental consequences for the environment, because of poor protective legislation that varies considerably from country to country. In addition, as mentioned earlier, global markets are prone to crisis as local conflicts, recessions and economic problems tend to spread across global networks. Indeed, the German sociologist Ulrich Beck (1944–2015) has called thinkers who blindly believe in globalisation and do not see the problems and risks involved "globalists" (Beck 1999).

Economic globalisation is also associated with cultural globalisation, as in a global market, products, ideas and people move faster transnationally than ever before. Spanish sociologist Manuel Castells (1996) has emphasised the importance of information and communication technology to the extent that he has appointed the current societies network societies. According to Castells, the development of the Internet has played a key role in economic globalisation, as the economy is today dependent on the rapid flow of information and knowledge. Castells talks about the network economy, where profits are amassed by players who control the information network or its core nodes, be they transnational corporations (e.g. Microsoft, Apple, Google, Facebook), states (e.g. United States, Northern European countries, China), cities or sub-regions (e.g. Silicon Valley of California, Citibank of London, Wall Street in New York) or individuals (e.g. Steve Jobs, Bill Gates, Mark Zuckerberg). In a network economy, "flex-timers" also thrive, adapting to the network's fluid and decentralised logic and learning to use it to their advantage. However, the largest number are unemployed "jobless" who are unable to participate in the network economy, for example, due to lack of resources. Castells' ideas about the network economy contribute to the changes that globalisation brings to national economies and economic structures.

The current populist wave that has risen in Europe and Asia in the late 20th century has often been seen as a reaction to globalisation (e.g. Panizza 2005; Hadiz & Chryssogelos 2017). Economic globalisation has brought about major structural changes in welfare states, where traditional industry and agriculture have been run down and relocated to low-cost countries. The economic structure in many Western countries has changed rapidly in a way that has led to unemployment, the need for retraining, flexibility requirements and labour market insecurity, as traditional industries have given way to new ICT-related sectors. The change has been fast, especially in male-dominated industries. This has cleared the way for populist movements that accuse specific enemies (elites, EU, immigrants) for workers' distress and promise certainty for their future (see Eatwell & Goodwin 2018). In my home country, for example, the foundation for the success of the populist right-wing Finns Party was laid in provinces where the paper and pulp industries shut down many major production facilities in the 2000s (Borg 2012).

Globalisation has also increased people's mobility. With the European Union's Schengen agreement, for example, allowing people to move fairly freely within an area of 26 countries, immigration and movement in traditional European nation states has dramatically increased. At the same time, conflicts, partly due to globalisation and partly for historical and geopolitical reasons, have created unprecedented refugee flows. For example, the war in Syria, the unrest in Iraq, the violent situation in Afghanistan, the aftermath of the revolutionary "Arab Spring" in North Africa 2011 and many local crises on the African continent led in 2015 to an avalanche of refugees not seen even during the Second World War in Europe. The sudden flow of people from different cultures, speaking, believing and behaving differently in the streetscape of welfare states, was a shock to some people that radical right populists have found easy to win over to their views.

The intercultural clashes caused by the increased movement of people, the threat of Islamist terrorism and its extreme nationalist or far right counter-movements combined with the huge number of people being helped, pose major economic and political challenges for national welfare states, and populist movements have played a key role in the politicisation of these challenges. Right-wing populist parties often have connections to extremists who push for a strictly nativist ideology and inflame the political atmosphere in liberal democracies (see Mudde 2019). This is why Germany, for example, defined AfD a possible threat to national security and therefore a target of surveillance in 2021. Populist logic emphasises confrontation with immigrants in often sharp, offensive and hateful ways. However, it is these affective and emotional experiences that act as a cement that unites supporters of right-wing populism and contribute to explaining the popularity of movements (Salmela & von Scheve 2017). At the same time, anti-globalisation left-wing radicalism has increased its support and various riots and violent clashes between extremists have become more common.

The rise of the Internet and social media in particular, has created platforms in which those who are afraid of the economic and cultural consequences of globalisation have been able to form like-minded communities. In Castells' (2007) terms, the Internet allows "mass-self communication", which transfers media power relations into a new constellation in which traditional mass media no longer have an unequivocal dominant position, and in principle anyone can reach significant audiences with their messages. In populist identifications, the social media play a key role, as they help, for example, right-wing populist nativist ideas find an echo chamber, even if the mainstream news media are critical of them (Krämer 2017). In a sense, this warrants Castells' (1996) earlier theory of the network economy, as these groups are often excluded from the network economy. On the other hand, the successful use of social media by right-wing populists shows that they are also "flex-timers" in the online society and are able to turn their precarious position into political activity, precisely through information and communication technologies. Thus, in addition to the fact that industrial restructuring, immigration and the deterioration of the welfare state have perhaps hit Western welfare states most directly, the widespread use of ICT may also explain why right-wing populist parties have been so successful in these countries during the 21st century.

Postmodernism

Talk about postmodernism emerged in the Western world in the 1970s and 1980s, suggesting that there had been a transition from modern to some new age. The term postmodernism was used in art as a reaction to modernism. Postmodernism in art was characterised by self-awareness, reflexivity, irony, references to other works of art and a kind of superficiality. Rather than relying on some deeper message or truth behind art, as was done in the ideal of modernist art, the proclaiming of truth was intended to be made visible to the public with various hints and ironic references. Instead of common and shared horizons of interpretation, postmodern art relied on individual and varied interpretations. Postmodernism manifested itself in the visual arts as playful collages that mixed different techniques, installations, conceptual art, performances and media art that transcended the boundaries of different art forms. It was also seen in literature and architecture in works that combined different styles and traditions that played with the audience's cultural knowledge.

In addition to art, many theorists began to speak more broadly about the postmodern era. Rather than an art style, postmodernism was, they said, a natural continuation or reaction to the currents of modern times. The postmodern era was characterised as, for example, "the death of great narratives", by which the French philosopher Jean-Francois Lyotard (1984) meant that meta-explanations such as religion, Marxism, capitalism, psychoanalysis and others no longer provided a definitive answer to a fragmented world, which was characterised instead by diverse micro-narratives. In addition to fragmentation, the postmodern era is characterised by superficiality or an emphasis on the surface in a radical sense. Jean Baudrillard (1998) described this "referring a sign to another sign" instead of some deeper meaning with the concept of simulacrum borrowed from Plato. According to Baudrillard, postmodernism means living in some kind of hyper-reality, where deeper meanings and truths are secondary or even disappear into the surface of the images that represent them. As an example of this, Baudrillard (1995) used, among other things, the Gulf War in 1991, when the United States invaded Kuwait to expel Saddam Hussein's Iraqi occupying forces. In the Western media, war looked like a video game rather than a human catastrophe. In the news images, tracer ammunition flew in the night sky, intelligent missiles showed a live video of their targets and fighter jets, combat helicopters and other warplanes glistened in the desert sun. In contrast, ruins, dead bodies and refugee flows were hardly seen in the news images.

Some theorists associated postmodern superficiality with the development of capitalism. For example, according to Fredric Jameson (1991), the impact of global financial capitalism is also reflected in a culture that replicates capitalist logic with its fragmented and superficial productions. In response to superficiality, culture produces pastiches, reprints of past masterpieces that respect and conform to "lost art" but do not attain the status of an independent or authentic work of art. Another defining feature of postmodern culture, according to Jameson, is nostalgia, a longing for the certainty of past times, great stories and truths. Nostalgia is evident both in arts and popular culture as a yearning for the good old days. Therefore, reproductions, sequels and references to well-known works are typical features of postmodern culture.

However, some scholars did not want to talk about postmodernism because, according to them, the term did not describe the era properly. For example, some thought that the term late modernity was more appropriate in the sense that it did not emphasise the transition to a completely new post-era (e.g. Fornäs 1995). Critics argued that the end of the 20th century had not entered a new era, but that the great currents of modern times – the emphasis on the individual subject, the central role of the nation-state, the importance of knowledge and the capitalist economy – continued as essential principles for Western culture and society. Rather, the importance of these traits was seen as increasingly emphasised, as a result of which there was also talk of accelerated modernisation, the hypermodern, or turbo-capitalism.

Sociologist Zygmunt Bauman (2000) used the term "liquid modernity" to emphasise that modern trends had drifted into a liquid space at the end of the 20th century. According to Bauman, the modern golden age was characterised by the pursuit of permanence and security and the slackening of the modern meant that uncertainty and continuous change infiltrated into the centre of work, education, human relations and social interaction. It is good to keep in mind, therefore, that concepts such as modern and postmodern are words developed afterwards to try to illustrate complex structural, social and cultural changes. The cultural currents do not end in an instant, they live together and intertwine. Even if we might live in a postmodern world, we are still quite modern, but "we have never been completely modern", as the anthropologist Bruno Latour (1993) has put it.

What is most essential in the period described as postmodern is the importance of the individual, the comprehensiveness of consumer culture, the mobilisation of social structures and the emphasis on the emotional. Bauman (2000) has called postmodern communities "cloakroom communities" because in the new form of community, personal ties and commitments are often momentary – as if a jacket is temporarily placed in a cloakroom. Thus, identities are not permanently fixed on the basis of communities and traditions but are also constantly on the move (Hall 1992). This has meant a new kind of politics that began to detach itself from modern ideologies and truths. While in the high modern age, mass parties were strengthened as institutions of representative democracy that conformed to the class structures of nation states, postmodernism began to break their foundations by bringing more individualist explanations to the centre of politics. British sociologist Anthony Giddens (1991, 214) described this change with the concept of life politics.

"Postmodern superficiality" was manifested in politics as the increased importance of individual politicians at the expense of the importance of the ideologies represented by political parties – as political performances entered the heart of politics. Individuality, affectivity and mobility describe the political life of the postmodern era. Postmodern theory thus contributes to the changes in democracy, such as the rise of audience democracy (Manin 1997) and the growing role of media in politics, the mediatisation of politics (Mazzoleni & Schulz 1999; Esser & Strömbäck 2014).

Postmodern politics is associated with declining political party engagement, politicisation of the personal and the increasing importance of identity politics. Some scholars see this as emancipatory because the fixed modern truths, disguised as universal, were very male- and Western-centred, thus fostering, for example, the unequal power division between genders, different groups of people and nations (Boyne & Rattansi 1990, 23–36). With the civil rights movement, feminism and the environmental movement, personal choices became truly political. Postmodern politics thus ventilated simple modern truths by bringing in diversity as the starting point for politics. This has inspired radical democratic theories that point to the problems of hegemonic politics returning to political institutions and emphasise the significance of genuine political contradictions arising from people's life worlds in context-specific ways (see Fenton 2016). For example, Laclau and Mouffe's ideas of populism as motives of the politicisation of social demands and the formation of political movements are related to such "post-foundational" theories (see Marchart 2007). On the other hand, critics of postmodernism have reminded us of the downside of a new kind of uncertainty: an increasing feeling of insignificance and exclusion because of the relativistic value landscape (e.g. Bauman 2000; Beck 1992).

The wave of new populism that emerged in the late 20th century can be considered postmodern in many ways. First, the postmodern environment provides a fertile ground for populist identifications. The loosening of traditional structures, the emphasis on individuality and the growing importance of affective identity politics erode the appeal of political parties based on traditional class structures and make populist movements relying on momentary political articulations attractive for identification. Populist movements can be seen as a kind of party politics that succeeds in appealing to people's emotional longing for group identity, often more effectively than traditional parties.

Second, new populism was a reaction to the challenges posed by postmodern nation states, politics and culture. Populism presents clarity and simple truths at a time when uncertainty is overwhelming and clear answers to political questions are difficult to find. New populism resorts to the longing for the heartland favoured by modern agrarian populism (Taggart 2000), where the answers can be found in the nation's happy past that is imagined as intact. In particular, nationalist right-wing populism is characterised by a nostalgic longing for the past, which is typical in postmodern culture (cf. Jameson 1991). Nationalism, nativism and simple enemy images bring clarity to a complex world. Multiculturalism is opposed because it complicates clear national values and tastes. Sometimes new populist movements even make demands on cultural life, such as the Finns Party in their 2011 parliamentary election manifesto, in which they explicitly opposed postmodernism and supported national romantic art.

Third, new populism is often ideologically "thin" or vague. Because populism is primarily about the political identification in which "forgotten people" are set against some other groups of people – elites, immigrants, minorities – populism itself does not form a strong ideology (Laclau 2005). Rather, it utilises, combines and modifies existing ideologies in a very postmodern way when needed and depending on the context (Stanley 2008). In this way, populism can momentarily articulate, that is, bring together, very different social demands and ideological trends, which can even traditionally contradict each other (Laclau 1977). In Bulgaria, for example, the populist Ataka party has emerged at the same time, depending on one's point of view, either as a far-right nationalist movement or as a far-left socialist party (see Ghodsee 2008). Populism thus forms a kind of postmodern collage in the field of politics, a patchwork which differs from the monochromatic ideology of the traditional left-right division. Populism represents liquid modernity as an empty signifier of a kind of political simulacrum. In fact, the secret behind the success of populism is that it is a postmodern way of resisting postmodernism: the current wave of populism is thoroughly postmodern.

Conclusion

Populism after the pandemic and Trump?

The future of populism looks different depending on how populism is understood. If populism is defined as a process of political self-understanding, identity formation and political confrontation, there will always be populism. In this sense, populism is an integral part of politics. If, on the other hand, populism is defined by particular political movements or ideologies, it will be more difficult to predict the future of populism, because the popularity of political movements and ideologies is connected to specific contexts. Seen in this way, the future of populism depends, among other things, on the manifestations of the nation-state, globalisation and postmodernism in local political contexts. It is also not appropriate to forget the importance of the media, which varies with changes in political cultures, media systems and communication technologies.

Populism, understood as a process of political identification has existed as long as modern politics has existed. Such populism will also exist as long as human societies organise their decision-making within a system understood as democracy. In this sense, populism is truly an integral part of democracy. According to Canovan (1999), populism arises from the internal tension of democracy between the ideal or promise of civil society and the institutional structures of democracy. Populism appeals to the disappointment that the day-to-day running of representative democracy through political parties, governments and governing institutions is often brought about from the perspective of civil society. When party politics does not enjoy enough public confidence, populism comes into play. Populism is a sort of path to political communality and often serves as a pathway in the early stages of new parties. Many individual politicians also use a populist style to attract attention and gain support.

Populism is always constructed in historical and local contexts, because the means, values and ideologies by which "the people" and

DOI: 10.4324/9781003267539-7

its enemies are defined depend on the particular context. Therefore, for example, Latin America's political history, social systems, media and geopolitical situation have usually encouraged different (left-wing, leader-centred) populism than in Western European consensus-based multi-party democracies, where nativist and party-centred right-wing populism has been more prevalent. On the other hand, the power of the global market economy, competition between states in the global market, international institutions and organisations such as the UN, IMF and WTO, geopolitical arrangements between states and the spread of information and communication technology place populism beyond national contexts.

In such an environment, populism spreads, and is deliberately spread, from one country to another. Political actors are modelling on each other across national borders, and some "third parties" deliberately want to confuse the national political fields by supporting populist movements financially or by promoting populist-friendly online campaigns and communities. Populism is part of the current information struggle between states and various factions, which seeks to create the most favourable climate of opinion for itself and to try to damage the unity of their "enemies". The logic of social media fits this purpose very well, as it specifically supports emotional community building through strong confrontations by populist means (see Engesser et al. 2017; Hatakka 2019).

In a way, populism has served a response to the crisis of the welfare state, globalisation and postmodernism and has taken different forms depending on national contexts. The response of nativist right-wing populism to these challenges has been an imagined longing for the lost "heartland" of the nation-state, building a wall around the nation and a rejection of people and influences from elsewhere. In economic terms, this has been seen, for example, in the proliferation of protectionist policies, such as the import duties and tariffs imposed by Donald Trump, and in the backlash they caused for the neoliberal global economy, which were discussed in the spring of 2018 as an emerging trade war. In foreign policy, the result has been a tightening of legislation on immigration, migration, refugees and border control.

Domestically, right-wing populists have pushed for social benefits to be allocated primarily for native citizens and, more generally, the interests of the indigenous majority at the expense of minorities, leading to a strong political divide between liberal and conservative groups and to constitutional challenges in liberal democracies. At the extreme, right-wing populists have begun to change the mechanisms of the constitution that balance the power and support the equality of the people, trying to centralise power on themselves and seizing control of the media. In this way, the populist movement, which initially emerged as a "protest of the people", turns into an authoritarian regime, where power is concentrated merely on the leader and his associates. Such developments have been seen in Turkey and Hungary in the 2010s, and Poland was catching up with them at the end of the 2010s. Donald Trump tried to proceed with the same kind of strategy but collided with the strong checks and balances of the US liberal democratic system in 2020. The mistrust of politics opens a door for authoritarian populism (Norris & Inglehart 2019).

The left-wing populists' response to the crisis of the welfare state, globalisation and postmodernism has been quite similar to that of right-wing populists, but they define their enemies on non-ethnic grounds. In left-wing populism, the enemies of the "people" are both corrupt politicians and the economic elite of their own country, as well as supranational corporations in the business and financial worlds and market-controlling organisations outside the country's borders. The policy has been to disregard supranational economic regulation, to prioritise national economic interests and to strengthen the role of the state in relation to the market. At their best, left-wing populist reforms in Asia and Latin America, for example, have initially succeeded in delivering greater prosperity for citizens, but these movements have also tended to turn into power-centred authoritarian regimes, such as Hugo Chávez's presidency in Venezuela (see Salojärvi 2016). As a result, the country's debt and financial problems in the international economy often deepen the strain on their international relations. The final result can be a systemic crisis or outright chaos, the consequences of which can be devastating for citizens.

A populist movement contributes to the revival of political life after a period of stagnation of a few decades. At the same time, it anticipates the redistribution and upheavals of the party field in many countries. New political parties are emerging and becoming successful through populist identifications. Once established, parties tend to lose their "populism" and be normalised in the party field or disappear. At present, however, it appears that populist movements are able to retain at least some of their populist logic even after rising to power (see Akkerman et al. 2016), demonstrating the resilience of populism. Because populism is not clearly an ideology, populist movements can exchange ideological anchors and enemies as needed if the old ones "wear out" and no longer convince their supporters. This has been the case, for example, with the Fidesz party led by Orbán, whose enemies have been found first in Hungary's own political elite, then in the

European Union and later among immigrants (see Kim 2020). In this way, populist movements are able to continually renew and appeal to their supporters by keeping some of the initial antagonism at the heart of political identification but changing the focus of the confrontation according to the moment.

In two-party systems or political systems that are strongly based on the confrontation between two blocs, the expansion of populism into a system-wide principle is more likely than in consensus-seeking multi-party systems (cf. Palonen 2009). Furthermore, in countries where the tradition and institutions of liberal democracy are young or otherwise weak, populism is more likely to turn to authoritarian rule than in countries with a strong tradition of liberal democracy (see Mudde & Kaltwasser 2012b). This is because in the latter, the institutions and securing mechanisms that maintain liberal democracy (such as the constitution, the judicial system, the opposition, the bureaucracy, the media) are so strong that it is difficult for an individual political actor to gain such an authoritarian position. In the old liberal democracies, the institutions of democracy also tend to enjoy the strong support of the majority of the people. Historically, in southern Europe and Anglo-American political culture, conflicts and confrontations have been generally more common than, for example, in consensus-seeking democracies in northern and central Europe, and therefore have made populism a normal part of politics in the former but rather an exception in the latter. However, 21st-century populism has not led to authoritarian regimes in either of them so far even if Donald Trump tried to push his regime towards authoritarian concept.

It is hard to believe that phenomena framing populism, such as the global transformations of the economy and industry, the growing awareness of other countries and cultures because of the Internet, or migration, would radically decrease or disappear in the near future. The major global challenge, climate change, makes these mega trends even more topical than before during the 2020s. Therefore, there are still good conditions for the emergence and strengthening of current populist movements. The country context, then, affects what forms populism eventually takes. Particularly in liberal democracies, various counter-movements opposing successful right-wing populist parties or the extremist movements linked to them have been launched, and the whole political system has become more confrontational than before. In this sense, it can be argued that the "populist Zeitgeist" has also spread to political systems that have been fairly enduring and consensus seeking for decades (Mudde 2004). This is why the first two decades of the 21st century can be called even the age of populism

(Krastev 2011). However, two contextual parameters shook political life significantly in 2020 and therefore also affected the future of populism around the world, namely the COVID-19 pandemic and the fall of Donald Trump.

In January 2020, China announced a new virus spreading especially in the Wuhan region of the country, which appeared very infectious and dangerous. The virus was called Corona and the serious disease it causes is COVID-19 that during February and March spread a global pandemic. About 80 million infections and 1.8 million deaths were reported globally during the year 2020 (WHO 2021). The countries that suffered most in proportion to the population were the United States and Brazil in the Americas and Italy, France, Spain, the UK, Belgium and Sweden in Europe. The number of infections was also high in Russia and India. The pandemic caused shattering effects on the mobility and freedom of people, while nation states closed their borders and set up lockdowns to protect their citizens and health care systems that, in many countries, were about to collapse under the flood of seriously ill people. The national and international restrictions also had a remarkable economic influence, because lockdowns cut down significantly on travelling, accommodation, restaurant and cultural businesses and also reduced international trade. This challenged the hegemony of neoliberal and monetarist financial political doctrine of the 21st century almost overnight, when individual nation states and the European Union decided to respond to the economic shock with exceptionally generous boosting and reflation (see Anderson et al. 2020).

The economic and political shock of COVID-19 pandemic also influenced populism. One may claim that the rather continuous triumph of populist political identifications and movements during the first two decades of the 21st century faced their first real break with the pandemic. However, the consequences of the pandemic to populism vary depending on the context. Furthermore, the ultimate political repercussions of the pandemic cannot properly be analysed until the disease has been defeated. However, preliminary mappings of the populism/pandemic relationship were already carried out during the first wave of COVID-19 in spring 2020. The Populismus network, run by the Aristotle University in Thessaloniki, collected a large-scale report on immediate impressions of the topic in sixteen countries and five continents together with the Populism Research Group at Loughborough University (Katsambekis & Stavrakakis 2020). The Populism in Action project also published, among other things, quick analyses of populism/pandemic relationships in four European countries during 2020.

As populism and COVID-19 consequences vary according to the contexts, the main message of these reports has been that there are remarkable contextual differences in populism/pandemic relationships between the countries. Giorgios Katsambekis and Yannis Stavrakakis (2020, 6–8) conclude in their introduction of the above-mentioned report that the popularity of populist actors varies during the pandemic, and no general principle of their loss or success can be given. They also remind us that populist actors have reacted very differently to the pandemic in different countries, and one should not understate the role of specific ideologies such as nationalism and nativism in political actors' responses to the crisis in the name of populism. As a vague umbrella term populism does not necessarily explain the political acts of the pandemic, and vice versa the pandemic impacts the ideological articulations behind the populist identifications. It is also clear that the relationship between the health experts and political actors varies between different countries, and this also has an impact on populist identifications.

In general, right-wing populist leaders with strong authoritarian tendencies such as Donald Trump and the President of Brazil Jair Bolsonaro belittled and even denied the threat caused by COVID-19, especially in the beginning of the pandemic (de Barros 2020; Lowndes 2020). In this they opposed the international community and domestic health experts and authorities, exploited the traditional populist antagonism and appealed to those who felt themselves to be the underdogs of authorities or even believed in conspiracies in which they were misled by official experts. However, as the crisis continued and deepened and the real consequences of COVID-19 came out, the strategy did not strengthen the populist identifications but rather began to fracture the status of populist leaders. These leaders had to mainstream their policies because their main economical argument to resist lockdowns and other restrictions proved unworkable in the light of the dangers of the COVID-19 pandemic.

Some authoritarian populist actors such as Viktor Orbán and his Fidesz party in Hungary utilised the pandemic to push through their autocratic power by appealing to the need for strong law and order in the fight against COVID-19 (Kim 2020; Lowndes 2020). However, in most liberal democratic countries the populist actors had to give up their political antagonisms, because people realised that they had to struggle with the pandemic as a united force and supported the traditional decision-makers and authorities in the fight. The lockdowns also closed national borders, ironically replicating nationalist and nativist demands for stricter border control. These demands had previously been made by right-wing populist actors especially in the European Schengen area, where people were used to free travelling between the countries. Therefore, it seems that the pandemic temporarily weakened the appeal of right-wing populist identifications and strengthened the confidence in traditional politics in the liberal democracies during spring 2020.

However, as the crisis continued and the serious economic challenges it caused were realised in countries with strict restrictions, opposition to lockdowns and decision-makers again occurred. People started to get tired of restrictions and in many countries the downturn in the support of populist movements in opinion polls stopped when criticism against ruling political parties started to become louder during the second half of 2020. A clear link between anti-restriction and anti-vaccination campaigns and right-wing populist movements was indicated in several countries. Therefore, it is too early to say that the pandemic created a crucial turning point in the success of populist right-wing parties in liberal democracies. Some scholars estimate, for example, that the economic boosting promoted by the decision-makers during the pandemic will lead to increasing collaboration with traditional right-wing parties and right-wing populist actors after the pandemic which, in turn, may lead to the increasing normalisation of populist movements (e.g. Hatakka 2020).

In addition to the pandemic, the fall of Donald Trump in the US 2020 presidential elections was seen as a dramatic check to the global triumph of right-wing populism. There were some signs of counter-reactions towards right-wing populism in Europe already before the pandemic. There was, for example, a significant loss in votes for right-wing populist parties and victory for the liberal greens parties in the parliamentary elections in Switzerland and Austria in 2019 and less success for the radical right parties in European Parliamentary elections in 2019 than was predicted, but these could be seen as normal alternations between governing and opposition political actors. However, the loss of the incumbent US President with a clear margin was a new indication of the majority's will to resist the authoritarian right-wing populism of Donald Trump, accompanied by the surprising victory of the Democratic Party in the senate election in Georgia in the aftermath of the presidential elections. Thus, the liberal democracy of the United States succeeded in defending itself against the attacks of authoritarian populism with the help of a majority vote and political institutions. Even if Trump and his extreme followers continued their struggle after the elections, the "checks and balances" of the oldest modern democracy in the world demonstrated their power (see Mudde & Kaltwasser 2012a). As populist articulations travel across the borders, it is plausible that their counter-reactions also spread between liberal democracies. The moderate majority may get bored with continuous political confrontations and start to push to diminish political polarisations.

However, the election results and the majority's voice do not necessarily remove the original reasons that call for populist identifications by some parts of the population, namely feelings of insecurity and disappointment with traditional party politics. Populism serves as a method in appealing to the social demands of these groups and is therefore a powerful tool in politicising and mobilising people in times of economic, cultural and political uncertainty. Chantal Mouffe (2005b), who developed the radical democratic theory of populism with Ernesto Laclau as a general logic of political identification, has commented with concern that populist articulations in so many cases at the beginning of this millennium have been linked to the hostile exclusion of others on ethnic grounds. Such populism leads to hatred and confrontations that do not take society forward. Instead of the "agonism" of the polyphonic coexistence of different societal interests called for by Mouffe (2002), the result is antagonism, which can have devastating social consequences. The conversion of populism into authoritarian regimes in some countries, suppressing the pluralism of the people, ideologies and voices, raises fears of the strengthening of totalitarian and extremist nationalist regimes such as the 1930s' Fascist and Nazi mass movements.

Since populism is contingently constructed in specific contexts and times, it is to be hoped that the context of populism in the 21st century would be decisively different from that in the 1930s. One must believe that at least in established liberal democracies, political systems do not collapse because of populism, but that populism acts as a means of politicisation that evokes democracy, highlights the social pain spots of the time and reshapes the party field to better meet the demands of citizens. If this is the future or not, depends on our capability to solve the global crises caused by the COVID-19 pandemic and climate change in a way that the majority of people living in democracies will trust in the democratic system and feel that their needs and demands are heard and taken into account in political decision-making. In this the role of media and communication will be essential.

For the first time in their history, the US-originated social media giants such as Facebook and Twitter closed the accounts of the political leader of the nation state during the violent aftermath of Donald Trump's defeat in the 2020–2021 presidential elections. However necessary that signal was, the procedure does not solve the problem of social media's algorithmic logic and emotional appeal in polarising community construction. On the contrary, the act appears dangerous and arbitrary with regard to the importance of social media as a forum for serious political opposition in both authoritarian contexts as well as in liberal democracies. Therefore, the only reasonable solution to the problem seems to be the democratic regulation of social media based on the law and carried out by the platforms themselves. In this way the content aiming at hatred and violence against individuals or particular groups is effectively eliminated and community building on these bases is restricted by their algorithms. Only in this way can social media fulfil their utopian functions as a platform for democratic pluralism and serve as a forum for political identifications promoting progressive social changes rather than authoritarian tendencies (cf. Fenton 2016).

References

Aalberg, Toril & Esser, Frank & Reinemann, Carsten & Strömbäck, Jesper & De Vreese, Claes (eds.) (2017) *Populist political communication in Europe*. New York: Routledge.

Adams, James & Clark, Michael & Ezrow, Lawrence & Glasgow, Garrett (2004) Understanding change and stability in party ideologies: Do parties respond to public opinion or to past election results? *British Journal of Political Science* 34:4, 589–610.

Adorno, W. Theodor & Frenkel-Brunswik, Else & Levinson, Daniel J. (1950) *The authoritarian personality*. New York: Harper & Brothers.

Akkerman, Tjitske (2011) Friend or foe? Right-wing populism and the popular press in Britain and the Netherlands. *Journalism* 12:8, 931–945.

Akkerman, Tjitske & de Lange, Sarah L. & Rooduijn, Matthijs (eds.) (2016) *Radical right-wing populist parties in Western Europe: Into the mainstream?* New York: Routledge.

Albertazzi, Daniele & McDonnell, Duncan (eds.) (2008) *Twenty-first century populism*. Basingstoke & New York: Palgrave Macmillan.

Albertazzi, Daniele & McDonnell, Duncan (2015) *Populist in power*. New York: Routledge.

Allern, Sigurd & Pollack, Ester (2016) Nordic political scandals – Frequency, type and consequences. In Mark Ludwig & Thomas Schierl & Christian von Sikorski (eds.) *Mediated scandals*. Köln: Halem, 146–163.

Althusser, Louis (1971) Ideology and ideological state apparatuses. In Louis Althusser (ed.), *Lenin and philosophy and other essays*. Translated by Ben Brewster. London: NLB, 121–176.

Ampuja, Marko (2012) *Theorizing globalization: A critique of the mediatization of social theory*. Leiden: Brill.

Anderson, Benedict (1983) *Imagined communities: Reflections and the origin and spread of nationalism*. London: Verso.

Anderson, Julia & Bergamini, Enrico & Brekelmans, Sybrand & Cameron, Aliénor & Darvas, Zsolt & Domínguez Jiménez, Marta & Lenaerts, Klaas & Midões, Catarina (2020) *The fiscal response to the economic fallout from the coronavirus*. Brussels: Bruegel.

Arditi, Benjamin (2005) Populism as internal periphery of democratic politics. In Francisco Panizza (ed.) *Populism in the mirror of democracy*. London: Verso, 72–98.

Arditi, Benjamin (2010) Populism is hegemony is politics? On Ernesto Laclau's On Populist Reason. *Constellations: An International Journal of Critical & Democratic Theory* 17:3, 488–497.

Aristotle (2004) *Rhetoric*. Translated by W. Rhys Roberts. New York: Dover Publications.

Aslanidis, Paris (2016) Is populism an ideology? A refutation and a new perspective. *Political Studies* 64:1, 88–104.

Bal, Mieke (2002) *Travelling concepts in the humanities: A rough guide*. Toronto: University of Toronto Press.

Bale, Tim & Kessel, Stijn van & Taggart, Paul (2011) Thrown around with abandon? Popular understandings of populism as conveyed by the print media: A UK case study. *Acta Politica* 46:2, 111–131.

Barros, Thomas Zicman de (2020) 4. Brazil. In Giorgios Katsambekis & Yannis Stavrakakis (eds.) *Populism and the pandemic: A collaborative report*. Thessaloniki: Populismus, 18–20.

Bartlett, Jamie & Birdwell, Jonathan & Littler, Mark (2011) *The new face of digital populism*. London: Demos.

Baudrillard, Jean (1995) *The Gulf War did not take place*. Indiana, US: Indiana University Press.

Baudrillard, Jean (1998 [1981]) Simulacra and simulations. In Mark Poster (ed.) *Jean Baudrillard: Selected writings*. Cambridge/Oxford: Polity, 169–187.

Bauman, Zygmunt (2000) *Liquid modernity*. Cambridge: Polity Press.

Bay, Ann-Helen & Finseraas, Henning & West Pedersen, Axel (2013) Welfare dualism in two Scandinavian welfare states: Public opinion and party politics. *West European Politics* 36:1, 199–220.

Beck, Ulrich (1992) *Risk society: Towards a new modernity*. London: Sage.

Beck, Ulrich (1999) *What is globalization?* Cambridge: Polity Press.

Billig, Michael (2001) Humour and hatred: The racist jokes of the Ku Klux Klan. *Discourse & Society* 12:3, 267–289.

Boomgaarden, Hajo G. & Vliegenthart, Rens (2007) Explaining the rise of anti-immigrant parties: The role of news media content. *Electoral Studies* 26:2, 404–417.

Borchers, Callum (2016) Yes, Donald Trump has been good for the media business. *The Washington Post* 25.10.2016.

Borg, Sami (2012) *Muutosvaalit 2011*. Helsinki: Oikeusministeriö.

Bos, Linda & Van Der Brug, Wouter & De Vreese, Claes (2011) How the media shape perceptions of right-wing populist leaders. *Political Communication* 28:2, 182–206.

Bowman, Paul (2007) The disagreement is not one: The populisms of Laclau, Rancière and Arditi. *Social Semiotics* 17:4, 540–545.

Boyne, Roy & Rattansi, Ali (1990) *Postmodernism and society*. London: Macmillan.

Brown, Katy & Mondon, Aurelion (2020) Populism, the media, and the mainstreaming of the far right: *The Guardian*'s coverage of populism as a case study. *Politics* 41:3, 279–295.

Canovan, Margaret (1981) *Populism*. London: Junction.

Canovan, Margaret (1999) Trust the people! Populism and the two faces of democracy. *Political Studies* 47:1, 2–16.

Canovan, Margaret (2005) *The people*. Cambridge: Polity Press.

Castells, Manuel (1996) *The rise of the network society*. Oxford: Blackwell.

Castells, Manuel (2007) Communication, power and counter-power in the network society. *International Journal of Communication* 1, 238–266.

Cerny, Philip G. (1997) Paradoxes of the competition state: The dynamics of political globalization. *Government and Opposition* 32:2, 251–274.

Chadwick, Andrew (2013) *The hybrid media system: Politics and power*. Oxford: Oxford University Press.

Couldry, Nick (2008) Mediatization or mediation? Alternative understanding of the emergent space of digital storytelling. *New Media & Society* 10:3. 373–391.

Couldry, Nick & Hepp, Andrew (2017) *The mediated construction of reality*. New York: Wiley.

Curran, Giorel (2004) Mainstreaming populist discourse: The race-conscious legacy of neo-populist parties in Australia and Italy. *Patterns of Prejudice* 38:1, 37–55.

Dean, Jonathan & Maiguashca, Bice (2020) Did somebody say populism? Towards a renewal and reorientation of populism studies. *Journal of Political Ideologies* 25:1, 11–27.

De Ipola, Emilio (1983) *Ideología y discurso populista*. Buenos Aires: Folios.

De la Torre, Carlos (ed.) (2019) *Routledge handbook of global populism*. London: Routledge.

Eatwell, Roger & Goodwin, Matthew (2018) *National populism: The revolt against liberal democracy*. London: Penguin Random House.

Engesser, Sven & Ernst, Nicole & Esser, Frank & Büchel, Florin (2017) Populism and social media: How politicians spread fragmented ideology. *Information, Communication and Society* 20:8, 1109–1126.

Elmgren, Ainur (2015) The Nordic ideal: Openness and populism according to the Finns Party. In Norbert Götz & Carl Marklud (eds.) *The paradox of openness: Transparency and participation in Nordic cultures of consensus*. Leiden: Brill, 91–119.

Ernst, Nicole & Engesser, Sven & Büchel, Florin & Blassnig, Sina & Esser, Frank (2017) Extreme parties and populism: An analysis of Facebook and Twitter across six countries. *Information, Communication and Society* 20:9, 1347–1364.

Esping-Anderssen, Gøsta (1999) *Social foundations of post-industrial economies*. Oxford: Oxford University Press.

Esser, Frank & Stepinska, Agnieszka & Hopmann, David Nicolas (2017) Populism and the media: Cross-national findings and perspectives. In Toril Aalberg & Frank Esser & Carsten Reinemann & Jesper Strömbäck & Claes De Vreese (eds.) *Populist political communication in Europe*. New York: Routledge, 365–380.

Esser, Frank & Strömbäck, Jesper (eds.) (2014) *Mediatization of politics: Understanding the transformation of Western democracies*. Hampshire: Palgrave Macmillan.

Fenton, Natalie (2016) *Digital, political, radical*. Cambridge: Polity Press.

Fiske, John (1992) Popularity and the politics of information. In Peter Dahlgren & Colin Sparks (eds.) *Journalism and popular culture*. London: Sage, 45–63.

Fraser, Nancy (1992) Rethinking the public sphere: A contribution to the critique of actually existing democracy. In Graig Calhoun (ed.) *Habermas and the public sphere*. Cambridge: The MIT Press, 109–142.

Freeden, Michael (1996) *Ideologies and political theory: A conceptual approach*. Oxford: Clarendon Press.

Fornäs, Johan (1995) *Cultural theory and late modernity*. London: Sage

Fukuyama, Francis (1992) *The end of history and the last man*. London: Free Press.

Gaertner, Wulf (2006) *A primer in social choice theory*. Oxford: Oxford University Press.

Ghodsee, Kristen (2008) Left-wing, right-wing, everything: Xenophobia, neo-totalitarianism, and populist politics in Bulgaria. *Problems of Post-Communism* 55:3, 26–39.

Giddens, Anthony (1991) *Modernity and self-identity: Self and society in the late modern age*. London: Polity Press.

Glynos, Jason & Howarth, David (2007) *Logics of critical explanation in social and political theory*. London: Routledge.

Glynos, Jason & Stavrakakis, Yannis (2004) Encounters of the real kind: Sussing out the limits of Laclau's embrace of Lacan. In Simon Critchley & Oliver Marchart (eds.) *Laclau: A critical reader*. London: Routledge, 201–216.

Gramsci, Antonio (2011 [1947]) *Prison notebooks*. Translated by Joseph A. Buttigieg & Antonio Callari. New York: Columbia University Press.

Groshek, Jacob & Koc-Michalska, Karolina (2017) Helping populism win? Social media use, filter bubbles, and support for populist presidential candidates in the 2016 US election campaign. *Information, Communication & Society* 20:9, 1389–1407.

Goyvaerts, Jana & De Cleen, Benjamin (2020) Media, anti-populist discourse, and the dynamics of the populism debate. In Benjamin Krämer (ed.) *Perspectives on populism and the media – Avenues for research*. Baden Baden: Nomos, 83–108.

Guardino, Matt & Snyder, Dean (2012) The Tea Party and the crisis of neoliberalism: Mainstreaming new right populism in the corporate news media. *New Political Science* 34:4, 527–548.

Gürhanli, Halil (2018) Populism on steroids: Erdoğanists and their enemies in Turkey. In Urpo Kovala & Emilia Palonen & Maria Ruotsalainen & Tuija Saresma (eds.) *Populism on the loose*. Jyväskylä: University of Jyväskylä, 53–80.

Habermas, Jürgen (1989 [1962]) *The structural transformation of the public sphere*. Translated by Thomas Burger. Cambridge: The MIT Press.

Hadiz, Vedi R. (2016) *Islamic populism in Indonesia and the Middle East*. Cambridge: Cambridge University Press.

Hadiz, Vedi R. & Chryssogelos, Angelos (2017) Populism in world politics: A comparative cross-regional perspective. *International Political Science Review* 38:4, 399–411.

Hadiz, Vedi R. & Robinson, Richard (2017) Competing populisms in post-authoritarian Indonesia. *International Political Science Review* 38:4, 488–502.

Hall, Stuart (1992) The question of cultural identity. In Stuart Hall & David Held & Anthony G. McGrew (eds.) *Modernity and its futures*. London: Polity and Open University Press.

Hall, Stuart (1988) The toad in the garden: Thatcherism among the theorists. In Cary Nelsson & Lawrence Grossberg (eds.) *Marxism and interpretation of culture*. London: Macmillan, 35–57.

Hallin, Daniel C. & Mancini, Paolo (2004) *Comparing media systems: Three models of media and politics*. Cambridge: Cambridge University Press.

Hallin, Daniel C. & Mancini, Paolo (eds.) (2012) *Comparing media systems: Beyond the Western world*. Cambridge: Cambridge University Press.

Hameleers, Michael & Schmuck, Desirée (2017) It's us against them: A comparative experiment on the effects of populist messages communicated via social media. *Information, Communication & Society* 20:9, 1425–1444.

Harvey, David (2005) *A brief history of neoliberalism*. Oxford: Oxford University Press.

Hatakka, Niko (2017) When logics of party politics and online activism collide: The populist Finns Party's identity under negotiation. *New Media & Society* 19:12, 2022–2038.

Hatakka, Niko (2019) *Populism in the hybrid media system: Populist radical right online counterpublics interacting with journalism, party politics and citizen activism*. Turku: University of Turku.

Hatakka, Niko (2020) *The profiteers of fear? Right-wing populism and the COVID-19 crisis in Europe: Finland*. Bonn: Friedrich Ebert Stiftung.

Hatakka, Niko & Niemi, Mari K. & Välimäki, Matti (2017) Confrontational yet submissive: Calculated ambivalence and populist parties' strategies of responding to racism accusations in the media. *Discourse & Society* 28:3, 262–280.

Hawkins, Kirk A. & Kaltwasser, Cristóbal Rovira (2017) The ideational approach to populism. *Latin American Research Review* 52:4, 513–528.

Helander, Voitto (ed.) (1971) *Vennamolaisuus populistisena joukkoliikkeenä*. Hämeenlinna: Karisto.

Held, David & McGrew, Anthony (2002) *Globalization/Anti-globalization*. New York: Wiley.

Hennessy, Alistair (1969) Latin America. In Ghita Ionescu & Ernest Gellner (eds.) *Populism: Its meanings and national characteristics*. London: Weidenfeld and Nicolson, 28–61.

Herkman, Juha (2016) Construction of populism: Meanings given to populism in the Nordic press. *Nordicom Review* 37(Special Issue), 147–161.

Herkman, Juha (2017a) Articulations of populism: The Nordic case. *Cultural Studies* 31:4, 470–488.

Herkman, Juha (2017b) The life cycle model and press coverage of Nordic populist parties. *Journalism Studies* 18:4, 430–448.

Herkman, Juha (2018) Old patterns on new clothes? Populism and political scandals in the Nordic countries. *Acta Sociologica* 61:4, 341–355.

Herkman, Juha & Jungar, Ann-Cathrine (2021) Populism and media and communication studies in the Nordic countries. In Eli Skogerbø & Øyvind Ihlen & Nete Nørgaard Kristensen & Lars Nord (eds.) *Power, communication, and politics in the Nordic countries*. Nordicom: Gothenburg, 241–261.

Herkman, Juha & Matikainen, Janne (2016) Neo-populist scandal and social media: The Finnish Olli Immonen affair. In Camil Demirhan & Derya Cakir-Demirhan (eds.) *Political scandal, corruption, and legitimacy in the age of social media*. Pennsylvania: IGI Global, 1–24.

Herkman, Juha & Matikainen, Janne (2019) Right-wing populism, media and political scandal. In Howard Tumber & Silvio Waisbord (eds.) *The Routledge companion to media and scandal*. London: Routledge, 147–155.

Hindmoor, Anrew (2006) *Rational choice*. London: Palgrave Macmillan.

Hjarvard, Stig (2013) *The mediatization of culture and society*. London: Routledge.

Hobsbawm, Eric (1994) *The age of extremes: The short Twentieth century 1914–1991*. London: Penguin Group.

Hobsbawm, Eric & Ranger, Terence (eds.) (1983) *The invention of tradition*. Cambridge: Cambridge University Press.

Hofstadter, Richard (1969) North America. In Ghita Ionescu & Ernest Gellner (eds.) *Populism: Its meanings and national characteristics*. London: Weidenfeld and Nicolson, 9–27.

Horowitz, Shale & Browne, Eric (2004) Post-communist party systems: Institutions and ideologies. *APSA Conference Papers*, 1–25.

Ionescu, Ghita (1969) Eastern Europe. In Ghita Ionescu & Ernest Gellner (eds.) *Populism: Its meanings and national characteristics*. London: Weidenfeld and Nicolson, 97–121.

Ionescu, Ghita & Gellner, Ernest (eds.) (1969) *Populism: Its meanings and national characteristics*. London: Weidenfeld and Nicolson.

Jagers, Jan & Walgrave, Stefan (2007) Populism as political communication style: An empirical study of political parties' discourse in Belgium. *European Journal of Political Research* 46:3, 319–345.

Jameson, Fredric (1991) *Postmodernism, or, the cultural logic of late capitalism*. London: Verso.

Jenkins, Henry (2008) *Convergence culture: Where old and new media collide*. New York: New York University Press.

Jessop, Bob (2002) Liberalism, neoliberalism, and urban governance: A state-theoretical perspective. *Antipode: A Radical Journal of Geography* 34:3, 452–472.

Jungar, Ann-Cathrine (2017) *Populism i Norden: Från marginalen mot den politiska mittfrån*. Helsingfors: Tankesmedjan Agenda.

Jungar, Ann-Cathrine & Jupskås, Anders Ravik (2014) Populist radical right parties in the Nordic region: A new and distinct party family? *Scandinavian Political Studies* 37:3, 215–238.

Kaltwasser, Cristóbal Rovira & Taggart, Paul & Espejo, Paulina Ochoa & Ostiguy, Pierre (eds.) (2017) *The Oxford handbook of populism*. Oxford: Oxford University Press.

Katsambekis, Giorgos & Stavrakakis, Yannis (eds.) (2020) *Populism and the pandemic: A collaborative report*. Thessaloniki: Populismus.

Kim, Seongscheol (2020) 8. Hungary. In Giorgios Katsambekis & Yannis Stavrakakis (eds.) *Populism and the pandemic: A collaborative report*. Thessaloniki: Populismus, 29–30.

Klinger, Ulrike & Svensson, Jakob (2015) The emergence of network media logic in political communication: A theoretical approach. *New Media & Society* 17:8, 1241–1257.

Koselleck, Reinhart (1989) Linguistic change and the history of events. *The Journal of Modern History* 61:4, 649–666.

Krämer, Benjamin (2014) Media populism: A conceptual clarification and some theses on its effects. *Communication Theory* 24:1, 42–60.

Krämer, Benjamin (2017) Populist online practices: The function of the Internet in right-wing populism. *Information, Communication & Society* 20:9, 1293–1309.

Krastev, Ivan (2011) The age of populism: Reflections on the self-enmity of democracy. *European View* 10:1, 11–16.

Kriesi, Hanspeter & Pappas, Takis (eds.) (2015) *European populism in the shadow of the Great Recession*. Colchester: ECPR Press.

Krotz, Friedrich (2007) The meta-process of "mediatization" as a conceptual frame. *Global Media and Communication* 3:3, 256–260.

Lacan, Jacques (1977) *Écrits: A selection*. New York: Norton.

Laclau, Ernesto (1977) *Politics and ideology in Marxist theory*. London: Verso.

Laclau, Ernesto (2005) *On populist reason*. London: Verso.

Laclau, Ernesto & Mouffe, Chantal (1985) *Hegemony & socialist strategy: Towards a radical democratic politics*. London: Verso.

Latour, Bruno (1993) *We have never been modern*. Cambridge, Massachusetts: Harvard University Press.

Leconte, Cécile (2010) *Understanding Euroscepticism*. Basingstoke: Palgrave Macmillan.

Leconte, Cécile (2015) From pathology to mainstream phenomenon: Reviewing the Euroscepticism debate in research and theory. *International Political Science Review* 36:3, 250–263.

Levitsky, Steven & Loxton, James (2012) Populism and competitive authoritarianism: The case of Fujimori's Peru. In Cas Mudde & Cristóbal Rovira Kaltwasser (eds.) *Populism in Europe and Americas: Threat or corrective for democracy?* Cambridge: Cambridge University Press, 160–181.

Lochocki, Timo (2017) *The rise of populism in Western Europe: A media analysis on failed political messaging*. New York: Springer.

Lowndes, Joseph (2020) 16. United States of America. In Giorgios Katsambekis & Yannis Stavrakakis (eds.) *Populism and the pandemic: A collaborative report*. Thessaloniki: Populismus, 53–56.

Lyotard, Jean-Francois (1984) *The postmodern condition: A report on knowledge*. Minnesota: University of Minnesota Press.

MacRae, Donald (1969) Populism as an ideology. In Ghita Ionescu & Ernest Geller (eds.) *Populism: Its meanings and national characteristics*. London: Weidenfeld and Nicolson, 153–165.

Manin, Bernard (1997) *The principles of representative government*. Cambridge: Cambridge University Press.

Marchart, Oliver (2007) *Post-foundational political thought: Political difference in Nancy, Lefort, Badiou and Laclau*. Edinburgh: Edinburg University Press.

Mazzoleni, Gianpietro (2008) Populism and the media. In Daniele Albertazzi & Duncan McDonnell (eds.) *Twenty-first century populism: The spectre of Western European democracy*. Hampshire: Palgrave Macmillan, 49–64.

Mazzoleni, Gianpietro (2014) Mediatization and political populism. In Frank Esser & Jesper Strömbäck (eds.) *Mediatization of politics: Understanding the transformation of Western democracies*. Basingstoke & New York: Palgrave Macmillan, 42–56.

Mazzoleni, Gianpietro & Schulz, Winfried (1999) Mediatization of politics: A challenge for democracy? *Political Communication* 16:3, 247–261.

Mazzoleni, Gianpietro & Stewart, Julianne & Horsfield, Bruce (eds.) (2003) *The media and neo-populism: A contemporary comparative analysis*. Westport, CT: Praeger.

McGuigan, Jim (1992) *Cultural populism*. London: Routledge.

Mény, Yves & Surel, Yves (eds.) (2002) *Democracies and the populist challenge*. Basingstoke: Palgrave.

Meyer, Thomas (2002) *Media democracy: How the media colonize politics*. Cambridge: Polity Press.

Minogue, Kenneth (1969) Populism as a political movement. In Ghita Ionescu & Ernest Geller (eds.) *Populism: Its meanings and national characteristics*. London: Weidenfeld and Nicolson, 197–211.

Moffitt, Benjamin (2016) *The global rise of populism: Performance, political style, and representation*. Stanford: Stanford University Press.

Moffitt, Benjamin (2020) *Populism. Key concepts in political theory*. Cambridge: Polity.

Moffitt, Benjamin & Tormey, Simon (2014) Rethinking populism: Politics, mediatisation and political style. *Political Studies* 62:2, 381–397.

Morgan, Edmund S. (1988) *Inventing the people: The rise of popular sovereignty in England and America*. New York: W.W. Norton.

Mouffe, Chantal (2002) For an agonistic public sphere. In Meta Bauer et al. (eds.) *Democracy unrealized*. Ostfildern-Ruit: Hatje Cantz Publishers, 87–96.

Mouffe, Chantal (2005a) *On the political*. London: Routledge.

Mouffe, Chantal (2005b) The "end of politics" and the challenge of right-wing populism. In Francisco Panizza (ed.) *Populism in the mirror of democracy*. London: Verso, 50–71.

Mudde, Cas (2000) *The ideology of the extreme right*. New York: Manchester University Press.

Mudde, Cas (2004) The populist Zeitgeist. *Government and Opposition* 39:4, 542–563.

Mudde, Cas (2007) *Populist radical right parties in Europe*. Cambridge: Cambridge University Press.

Mudde, Cas (2017) Populism: An ideational approach. In Cristóbal Rovira Kaltwasser & Paul Taggart & Paulina Ochoa Espejo & Pierre Ostiguy (eds.) *The Oxford handbook of populism*. Oxford: Oxford University Press, 27–47.

Mudde, Cas (2019) *The far right today*. Cambridge: Polity Press.

Mudde, Cas & Kaltwasser, Cristóbal Rovira (2012a) Populism and (liberal) democracy: A framework for analysis. In Cas Mudde & Cristóbal Rovira Kaltwasser (eds.) *Populism in Europe and Americas: Threat or corrective for democracy?* Cambridge: Cambridge University Press, 1–26.

Mudde, Cas & Kaltwasser, Cristóbal Rovira (2012b) Populism: Corrective and threat to democracy. In Cas Mudde & Cristóbal Rovira Kaltwasser (eds.) *Populism in Europe and Americas: Threat or corrective for democracy?* Cambridge: Cambridge University Press, 205–222.

Mudde, Cas & Kaltwasser, Cristóbal Rovira (2017) *Populism: A very short introduction*. Oxford: Oxford University Press.

Müller, Jan-Werner (2016) *What is populism?* Philadelphia: University of Philadelphia Press.

Murdock, Graham (2020) Profits of deceit: Performing populism in polarized times. *European Journal of Cultural Studies* 23:6, 874–899.

Negrine, Ralph & Mancini, Paolo & Holtz-Bacha, Christina & Papathanassopoulos, Stylianos (eds.) (2007) *The professionalisation of political communication*. Changing Media, Changing Europe: Volume 3. Bristol, UK: Intellect.

Norris, Pippa & Inglehart, Ronald (2019) *Cultural backlash: Trump, Brexit, and authoritarian populism*. Cambridge: Cambridge University Press.

Palonen, Emilia (2009) Political polarisation and populism in contemporary Hungary. *Parliamentary Affairs* 62:2, 318–334.

Palonen, Kari (2003) Four times of politics: Policy, polity, politicking and politicization. *Alternatives* 28:2, 171–186.

Panizza, Francisco (ed.) (2005) *Populism in the mirror of democracy*. Verso: London.

Pappas, Takis S. (2019) *Populism and liberal democracy: A comparative and theoretical analysis*. Oxford: Oxford University Press.

Perelló, Gloria & Biglieri, Paula (2012) On the debate around Immanence and Transcendence. *Cultural Studies* 26:2–3, 319–329.

Plasser, Fritz & Ultram, Peter A. (2003) Striking a responsive chord: Mass media and right-wing populism in Austria. In Gianpietro Mazzoleni & Julianne Stewart & Bruce Horsfield (eds.) *The media and neo-populism: A contemporary comparative analysis*. Westport, CT: Praeger. 21–43.

Reinemann, Carsten & Matthes, Jörg & Sheafer, Tamir (2017) Citizens and populist political communication: Cross-National findings and perspectives. In Toril Aalberg et al. (eds.) *Populist political communication in Europe*. New York: Routledge, 381–394.

Reinemann, Carsten & Stanyer, James & Aalberg, Toril & Esser, Frank & De Vreese, Claes (eds.) (2019) *Communicating populism: Comparing actor perceptions, media coverage, and effects on citizens in Europe*. London: Routledge.

Rodan, Garry (2012) Competing ideologies of political representation in Southeast Asia. *Third World Quarterly* 33:2, 311–332.

Roodjuin, Matthijs (2014) The mesmerising message: The diffusion of populism in public debates in Western European media. *Political Studies* 62:4, 726–744.

Rosanvallon, Pierre (2008) *Counter-democracy: Politics in the age of trust*. Cambridge: Cambridge University Press.

Rydgren, Jens (2010) Radical right-wing populism in Denmark and Sweden: Explaining party system change and stability. *The SAIS Review of International Affairs* 30:1, 57–71.

Salmela, Mikko & von Scheve, Christian (2017) Emotional roots of right-wing political populism. *Social Science Information*. 56:4, 567–595.

Salojärvi, Virpi (2016) *The media in the core of political conflict: Venezuela during the last years of Hugo Chávez's presidency*. Helsinki: University of Helsinki.

Sartori, Giovanni (2005 [1976]) *Parties and party systems: A framework for analysis*. Colchester: ECPR Press.

Saussure, Ferdinand de (1960 [1916]) *Course in general linguistics*. Translated by Albert Reidlinger. London: Peter Owen.

Schumpeter, Joseph A. (1949) *Capitalism, socialism and democracy*. New York: Harper.

Shields, James (2014) The Front National: From systematic opposition to systemic integration? *Modern & Contemporary France* 22:4, 491–511.

Shils, Edward (1956) *The torment of secrecy*. London: William Heinemann.

Skogerbø, Eli & Ihlen, Øyvind & Kristensen, Nete Nørgaard & Nord, Lars (eds.) (2021) *Power, communication, and politics in the Nordic countries*. Nordicom: Gothenburg.

Stanley, Ben (2008) The thin ideology of populism. *Journal of Political Ideologies* 13:1, 95–110.

Stanyer, James (2007) *Modern political communication*. Cambridge: Polity.

Stewart, Angus (1969) The social roots. In Ghita Ionescu & Ernest Gellner (eds.) *Populism: Its meanings and national characteristics*. London: Weidenfeld and Nicolson, 180–196.

Stewart, Julianne & Mazzoleni, Gianpietro & Horsfield, Bruce (2003) Conclusion: Power to the media managers. In Gianpietro Mazzoleni & Julianne Stewart & Bruce Horsfield (eds.) *The media and neo-populism: A contemporary comparative analysis*. Westport, CT: Praeger, 217–236.

Stier, Sebastian & Posch, Lisa & Bleier, Arnim & Strohmaier, Markus (2017) When populists become popular: Comparing Facebook use by the right-wing movement Pediga and German political parties. *Information, Communication & Society* 20:9, 1365–1388.

Strömbäck, Jesper (2008) Four phases of mediatization: An analysis of the mediatization of politics. *The International Journal of Press/Politics* 13:3, 228–246.

Strömbäck, Jesper & Ørsten, Mark & Aalberg, Toril (eds.) (2008) *Communicating politics: Political communication in the Nordic countries*. Gothenburg: Nordicom.

Sumiala, Johanna (2013) *Media and ritual: Death, community and everyday life*. London: Routledge.

Syvertsen, Trine & Enli, Gunn & Mjøs, Ole J. & Moe, Hallvard (2014) *The media welfare state: Nordic media in the digital era*. Michigan: The University of Michigan Press.

Taggart, Paul (2000) *Populism*. Buckingham, UK: Open University Press.

Taggart, Paul (2002) Populism and the pathology of representative politics. In Yves Mény & Yves Surel (eds.) *Democracies and the populist challenge*. Basingstoke: Palgrave, 62–80.

Taggart, Paul & Szczerbiak, Aleks (2002) Europeanisation, Euroscepticism and party systems: Party-based Euroscepticism in the candidate states of Central and Eastern Europe. *Perspectives on European Politics and Society* 3:1, 23–41.

Taguieff, Pierre-André (2002) *L'Illusion populiste*. Paris: Berg International.

Thompson, B. John (1995) *The media and modernity: A social theory of the media*. Cambridge: Polity Press.

Thompson, B. John (2000) *Political scandal: Power and visibility in the media age*. Cambridge: Polity Press.

Thompson, Mark R. (2010) Populism and the revival of reform: Competing political narratives in the Philippines. *Contemporary Southeast Asia* 32:1, 1–28.

Van Dijck, Jose & Poell, Thomas (2013) Understanding social media logic. *Media and Communication* 1:1, 2–14.

Vesa, Juho (2016) *Päätöksenteon avoimuus ja medioituminen Suomen konsensus-demokratiassa*. Helsinki: Helsingin yliopisto.

Vincent, Louise (2011) Seducing the people: Populism and challenge to democracy in South Africa. *Journal of Contemporary African Studies* 29:1, 1–14.

Waisbord, Silvio & Amado, Adriana (2017) Populist communication by digital means: Presidential Twitter in Latin America. *Information, Communication & Society* 20:9, 1330–1346.

Walgrave, Stefaan & De Swert, Knut (2004) The making of the (Issues of the) Vlaams Blok. *Political Communication* 21:4, 479–500.

Walicki, Andrej (1969) Russia. In Ghita Ionescu & Ernest Gellner (eds.) *Populism: Its meanings and national characteristics*. London: Weidenfeld and Nicolson, 62–96.

Wettstein, Martin & Esser, Frank & Schulz, Anne & Wirz, Dominique S. & Wirth, Werner (2018) News media as gatekeepers, critics, and initiators of populist communication: How journalists in ten countries deal with the populist challenge. *The International Journal of Press/Politics* 23:4, 476–495.

WHO (2021) WHO Corona virus disease (Covid-19) dashboard. <https://covid19.who.int/> Uploaded on 10 January 2021.

Wiles, Peter (1969) A syndrome, not a doctrine. In Ghita Ionescu & Ernest Gellner (eds.) *Populism: Its meanings and national characteristics*. London: Weidenfeld and Nicolson, 166–179.

Williams, Raymond (1988) *Keywords: A vocabulary of culture and society*. London: Fontana.

Wodak, Ruth (2013) "Anything goes!" The Haiderization of Europe. In Ruth Wodak & Majid KhosraviNik & Brigette Mra (eds.) *Right-wing populism in Europe: Politics and discourse*. London: Bloomsbury, 23–37.

Wodak, Ruth (2015) *The politics of fear: What populist right-wing discourses mean?* London: Sage.

Worsley, Peter (1969) The concept of populism. In Ghita Ionescu & Ernest Gellner (eds.) *Populism: Its meanings and national characteristics*. London: Weidenfeld and Nicolson, 212–250.

Zaslove, Andrej (2008) Here to stay? Populism as a new party type. *European Review* 16:3, 319–336.

Žižek, Slavoj (1989) *The sublime object of ideology*. London: Verso.

Index